Corporate Tides

This book is dedicated to my friends and colleagues
Charlie Kiefer and Peter Senge

Corporate Tides

Redesigning the organization

Robert Fritz

Butterworth-Heinemann Ltd
Linacre House, Jordan Hill, Oxford OX2 8DP

 A member of the Reed Elsevier plc group

OXFORD   LONDON   BOSTON
MUNICH   NEW DELHI   SINGAPORE   SYDNEY
TOKYO   TORONTO   WELLINGTON

First published 1994

British Library Cataloguing in Publication Data
Fritz, Robert
  Corporate Tides: Redesigning the
  Organization
  I. Title
  658.4012

ISBN 0 7506 2149 4

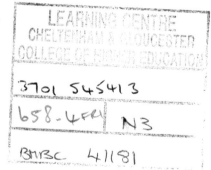

Composition by Scribe Design, Gillingham, Kent, UK.
Printed in Great Britain by Clays, St Ives plc

Contents

Preface

When Robert Craft asked Igor Stravinsky what he thought of music theory, the great composer answered 'Hindsight'. As usual, there was profound insight within Stravinsky's wit. Historically, the practice of writing music predates the theories that developed about it later. But insight was lost, and then students learned the theories first, and often confused practice with theoretical formula. This made it harder for them to learn how to compose music. There is much to be learned by Stravinsky's comment in contemporary organizational life.

With so many managerial theories abounding in today's organizational world we can become confused when theory *predates* practice. Many notions come more from the philosophical or abstract realms than pragmatic organizational reality. Such a theory can function as an ideal that one is asked to reach. As an ideal, it can be steeped in a purely conceptual frame that generates its own self-referential standards of measurements that have little to do with the successful ordering of an organization. How well we execute the theory can become more important than how well we run the company.

This book is filled with theory. But it is theory that has been developed over more than twenty years of hands-on practice in organizations. Practice has preceded theory, and theory has been put to the test over and over again. The theory has changed greatly from its first inception, and all the changes have come from our actual work in organizations developing or executing long-range strategy, understanding organizational complexity and the principles of structural design that were needed to accomplish real and lasting change.

You will find, however, that I do not refer to much of the work we have done within organizations. The reason for this is professional, for we have signed anti-disclosure agreements with all our major organizational clients. The stories we can't tell are fascinating and wonderful. Nonetheless, the stories that might have been told only illustrate the points that are made, rather than add new information. With the great success of the 'executive summary' form of communication that has become popular recently, many are finding that illustrating a point with 'war stories' is not necessary to understand the point. The ideas in this book have their antecedents in real organizational work, and the best way to penetrate the usefulness of this work is to put it to the test in your own organization.

The material contained in *Corporate Tides* is some of the most practical and effective insights about complex organizations I know. It translates well to the real world because it addresses structural causes rather than symptomatic-based prescriptions for behaviour, and because of that, structural redesign becomes a major factor in the organizational change effort. It has been put to the test, and it has passed with flying colours time and time again. It is reliable, practical and yet very different from many popular views about organizations. In an age of downsizing, organizational insecurity, increased fragmentation of companies, and the other hardships organizations have experienced, there is hope. But the hope lies in a different way of thinking and understanding, different from those that produced the current conditions. Let us penetrate the causes of organizational behaviour, policy design, decision-power distribution, and long-range strategy, armed with a new understanding and new ways of addressing change. That is the aim of this book.

Robert Fritz

Acknowledgements

There are many people who have contributed greatly to this book: my editor, Susan Allport; my friend and literary agent, Jacques de Spoelberch; my wife and colleague, Rosalind; Alan Mossman, for his work on the index; the staff at Technologies for Creating®, Inc., especially Robert Carlson and Karen Mathieu; our friends and colleagues at Chloe Cox Consultants Ltd (UK); and Butterworth-Heinemann's staff, in particular Tom McGorry. Thank you all!

1 Structure

Two faces of the organization

The modern organization is capable of accomplishing something quite extraordinary. It can be a vehicle for expressing that which is highest in the human spirit – our inclination to build, invent, explore, learn, and create. It provides us with the opportunity to join together and, through our union, to accomplish feats that would have been impossible individually. It harnesses the power of vast resources into a collective force that turns great vision into reality. It saves lives through scientific research and development, helps the world to communicate through technology, and it generates and distributes wealth through industry. It is a vital, civilizing force.

The people I know who work in organizations are industrious, sincere, and competent. They care about their companies – much more than they often want to admit. From senior management to the rank-and-file, there is a tremendous energy, talent, inventiveness, effort, and commitment filling the organization with new possibilities for the future.

Yet the organization also has its darker side. Sometimes it seems like an impersonal bureaucracy that is capable of tearing apart people's lives if deemed necessary, as has happened time and time again with the advent of downsizing. Chronic inefficiency squanders money, time, and talent. Political intrigues lead people to work against each other. Short-sightedness can defeat the organization's vision and purpose, and limit its success. The organizational hold on reality sometimes weakens to a point where no one seems to know, or even wants to know, what is going on. The organization can seem like a necessary evil that we must put up with if we are to create products and provide services to the world.

Given these very different faces of the organization, what is its future?

The elusive pursuit of change

There are two and only two possibilities for the future of organizations. Either they can be changed and improved or they are the way they are, and any attempts to change them will not work.

Some experts hold the view that organizational change *is* possible and a very worthwhile cause. Others have concluded that all efforts to change are superficial, that the best any of us can do is to accept the reality that organizations, by their very nature, are flawed. As in the old prayer, 'Lord, give me the strength to change what I can, accept what I can't, and have the wisdom to know the difference', many think that we must have the wisdom to accept reality for what it is – organizations can't be changed.

To these people, who have watched change effort after change effort hit their organizations over the years, nothing seems to work. They have seen it all, from T-groups, to management by objectives (MBO) to the latest in total quality management (TQM) and business re-engineering. They have seen excitement for each new system blossom then fade once the idea is put into practice. They have seen champions, systems, and slogans come and go while the organization remains unchanged.

These are the house sceptics. Their lack of enthusiasm for the next new system to appear is based on a wealth of previous experience that has taught them that change efforts consistently fail. If their scepticism is warranted, then not only are change efforts wasteful, they actually take people away from the real work of the company; they may be distracting and harmful. The January 1992 issue of the European journal *Training and Development* cites a study that researched the move toward Total Quality in European companies:

> In their quest for quality, many European companies are actually damaging their chances of improving their services and competitiveness according to the findings of a new report published by *The Economist* Intelligence Unit.
>
> The study, *Making quality work – lessons from Europe's leading companies* was conducted by consultants and researchers from

Ashridge Management College. George Binney, who led the study, says, 'Total Quality Programs – company-wide, training-led, add-ons to existing jobs – are, at best, ineffective. At worst, they inoculate the organization against real change'.

Binney is also scathing about the emphasis so many companies put on standards such as BS 5750 and ISO 9000. 'They are the bureaucracy of quality,' he says. 'They have a useful role to play, but to start with the standards is to put the cart before the horse.'

Is organizational change possible? That is truly a billion-dollar question given the enormous resources that organizations spend every year in attempts to promote change. People will pretend that change is working, at least for a while, and this is one of the major problems in evaluating the reality of organizational change. People who are in charge of the change make exaggerated claims. But the house sceptics are often right. Large-scale organizational-wide change efforts are rarely successful in the long run.

We want our organizations to be better than they are, for the sceptic as much as the 'believer'. But can they truly change? The sceptic's opinion is ignored by those who wish to improve the company. This is a mistake. We need to appreciate that the sceptic sees a pattern of failed attempts. While a new theory or system may be different in detail from all of the previous ones, to the sceptic, people, yet again, are putting their hopes in a false salvation. So now it is *the learning organization*, or *Total Quality*, or *re-engineering*. Next week, it will be something else.

Books like *In Search of Excellence* claim that particular companies hold keys to success, but these claims do not hold up to time and scrutiny. Five years after publication, management researchers went back to the companies cited in Peters and Waterman's famous book only to find that most of them no longer fulfilled the ideals for which they had been celebrated.

Propaganda hurts its own cause. Recently, I sat through a discussion by a panel of 're-engineering czars' who were gushing about all that they had accomplished in their various organizations. They were extremely hopeful and encouraging, and if I hadn't had clients in these very organizations, I would have been as taken in as many in the audience. In fact, the reality of the situation was radically different from their description. Perhaps the 'czars' were merely deceiving themselves, but time is not on their side, and truth will eventually out. Their claims only give the sceptics more ammunition for discrediting any hope of change.

Why is change so hard to accomplish, particularly when so many well-meaning people want it? It is because of the way change is approached. The focus of the change effort is typically on either *behaviour* or *systems* and not on the directly causal forces that determine how an organization operates – its underlying *structure*. If the wheels of our cars were out of alignment and pulled to the left, we would compensate by steering to the right whenever we wanted to drive straight. Our friends might suggest a behavioural change – 'You keep pulling the steering wheel to the right. What you should do is steer in a straight line!' We might take their advice only to find that we could not sustain it for long. In a similar way, organizations typically attempt to change behaviour without understanding the real cause of the current behaviour. If we do not address the cause, we will not be able to change behaviour – period.

A change of system in our analogy might lead our friends to give us different advice – 'First look down the road, and then pull the wheel to the left, and then to the right, and then...' We might become more efficient at executing our compensating strategy, but we will still have the same behavioural tendency – to pull to the right when we want to drive straight. The structure, not our good intentions, or how many other cars are able to steer straight, or our resolve, or even how good our process systems are will determine how we perform.

If we took our car to a garage and got our wheels aligned, our steering habits would change immediately. When we wanted to drive straight, we would steer straight. It wouldn't take any time to adopt the new behaviour. In this analogy, *a change of structure leads to a change of behaviour automatically and naturally.*

The guiding thought behind behavioural change is that we can transform our organizations if we act in new ways. Members of the organization are asked to adopt new concepts, beliefs, and actions. Decrees for proper behaviour are promoted in the form of 'value statements' or 'codes'. The Achilles' heel of these approaches is the notion that people act the way they do within organizations based primarily on their own individual choices. In fact, they usually do not. There are many structural forces in play that are not of the individual's own making: conflicting rewards and penalties, conflicts of loyalties, unclear direction, mixed messages, and so on.

If we could merely prescribe new behaviours for the members of an organization life would be a lot simpler than it is. Instead, we need to consider – as this book will do – *why* people act the way they do within our organizations. For unless we understand the causes of their behaviour, we cannot hope to change it.

The other type of change that organizations attempt is on the level of systems and procedures. Total Quality Management (TQM) is a good example. TQM is a superb concept. However, many companies have adopted it with great enthusiasm, only to abandon it later with great disappointment. The reasons many organizations have trouble implementing TQM, re-engineering, or other change systems for that matter is not because they are bad systems but because these systems are taken on manneristically within a dysfunctional organizational structure. Since organizational structural issues remain unaddressed, the new approach is adopted only superficially. Important questions about the values, philosophy, and organizational structural architecture have not been asked. In order to use such a system successfully a deeper thought process must pave the way. Serious questions must be considered. What is our *true* interest in quality products, quality management systems, or the forms of change? What do we hope to achieve? What is the relationship between the new system and our prime business strategy? If an organization is adopting a change system simply because 'It's good for us' or 'If we don't we will not be competitive' its motivation is on shaky ground.

Nothing short of real caring for quality methods, or other large-scale system processes, will lead to the type of commitment that is a prerequisite for such a vast change in management procedures. Any system that demands the degree of involvement as does TQM, re-engineering, or building a learning organization cannot succeed as a simple add-on to an organization that is unclear about its most fundamental dimensions – its purpose, values, vision, and especially its underlying structure. While some systems are certainly better than others, all change will fail unless it is on an essential *structural* level. And a system adopted for the wrong reason is doomed from the start.

Not many organizations realize the intellectual and managerial rigour required when attempting large-scale change. Instead of considered thought, we find a new form of pep-talk. TQM, re-engineering, organizational learning, core competencies, rah, rah, rah. All these approaches represent positive change in organizational thinking. But the true value often drowns in hype. Hype cannot sustain itself for ever. After years of success stories filling the management literature about various forms of change, a pattern of failed attempts is beginning to surface. Robert S. Kaufman, writing in MIT's *Sloan Management Review* (Fall, 1992), has described the condition many managers face:

> Your predicament as manager of a manufacturing revival is common: after years of educating yourself in the concepts of just-in-time and employee involvement, you launched an ambitious program in your company. After achieving dramatic productivity gains, you were convinced you were on the road to success. But the gains turned out to be only temporary, and now you're less optimistic. Employees are devoting less time to the program. Like failed initiatives of the past, it is being referred to with that terminal phrase, 'just another program.'
>
> You have tried all you can think of to revive the program, with little success. You are beginning to wonder whether you and your team have what it takes.

Motivated by problems within the organization, or in staying current with what's in vogue, many managers hope that a change of system will lead the organization to a metamorphosis. So they search for the perfect system they can adopt. But problem-driven action loses its momentum as soon as the situation improves, and changing management fads fade awfully fast.

An implication

There is a subtle assumption built into these kinds of motivations which has a devastating implication: that our reason to act is primarily *circumstantial*. At first, perhaps, there seems to be nothing amiss with this notion. Our earliest experiences have taught us to see our world as a stimulus which drives our reactions and responses. As children we quickly learned to assess any situation, particularly those concerning adults, and develop compensating strategies.

This kind of training is vital because when we are children our very survival may depend on our reactions and responses. Certainly a good deal of our training centred around learning the 'proper' responses in circumstances that concerned our physical well-being: crossing streets safely, for example. But too often we suffer from arrested development; we are left with one and only one premise about life: that our role is limited to compensating for changing circumstances. When this is the case, we are trapped by circumstances. We can think only in terms of past or present situations. If we consider the future at all, it is only to anticipate how circumstances might change so that we can organize our reactions and responses accordingly.

If we are trapped in this kind of thinking, circumstances, rather than our aspirations, are the most powerful force in our lives. We suffer an enormous invisible loss from this limitation. We lose touch with our *generative* faculties – the ability to envisage new and original possibilities that are born within the depth of our aspirations and are independent of the prevailing circumstances. We relinquish our ability to imagine, invent, explore, and bring into being creations that have never been thought of before, that would have been impossible to conceive of if we were merely extrapolating from previous trends.

While many companies *speak* about vision they *think* in terms of reactions and responses. They take pride in their ability to respond quickly to the marketplace or to their customers. They describe themselves as dedicated problem solvers. They study systems of 'benchmarking', which drives their focus towards convention rather than invention. While common practice is always good to scrutinize, this should only contribute to a considered thought process. But for many companies true thought is abandoned in favour of new prescriptions for behaviours that, while giving the illusion of strategic thinking, only fail to generate real strategy.

When Japanese companies develop a new competitive advantage, such as manufacturing flexibility, Western companies rush to catch up. Were the Japanese simply reacting to marketplace demands or were they *inventing* new markets based on their vision for the future? The real competitive edge is found in the way people *generate* the future, not in how well they respond to the present. Opportunities are lost when we simply copy new trends in a 'me too' response.

In a 1989 *Harvard Business Review* article entitled 'Strategic intent', Gary Hamel and C. K. Prahalad, two of the world's leading authorities on corporate strategy, wrote:

> Too many companies are expending enormous energy simply to reproduce the cost and quality advantages their global competitors already enjoy. Imitation may be the sincerest form of flattery, but it will not lead to competitive revitalization. Strategies based on imitation are

transparent to competitors who have already mastered them. Moreover, successful competitors rarely stand still. So it is not surprising that many executives feel trapped in a seemingly endless game of catch-up – regularly surprised by the new accomplishments of their rivals . . .

The lesson is clear: assessing the current tactical advantages of known competitors will not help you understand the resolution, stamina, and inventiveness of potential competitors. Sun-tzu, a Chinese military strategist, made the point 3,000 years ago: 'All men can see the tactics whereby I conquer,' he wrote, 'but what none can see is the strategy out of which great victory is evolved.'

A reactive/responsive orientation in which prevailing circumstances dominate the organizational thought process will not succeed in the fierce global rivalries of today's world. The only orientation with any chance is one that is *generative*.

Western companies cannot prevail if they are wedded to the circumstantial thought processes of the past, for the only competitive advantage that ultimately matters is found in organizational aspiration, imagination, values, and structure. So what has to change if the organization is to participate in today's world?

What has to change?

Change is hard to accomplish because people do not understand what really drives their organizations. The thinking goes like this: 'Here is the problem, what should we do about it?' Little attention is given to understanding why the conditions are the way they are, except to know enough to begin to take action to change the conditions. A thorough understanding of why things are the way they are is a different focus from the impulse to take action immediately. However, we as managers are used to taking action, so we react or respond to symptoms rather than research the more important underlying causal factors that create the current conditions. In order to explore these causal factors we must begin to think on an entirely revolutionary platform – that of *structure*.

Twenty years ago I made the following essential discovery: *the inherent structure of anything will determine its behaviour*. This statement will have little meaning for you right now. But I promise you this: when you understand just what structure is, what it does, and why it is so important, you will be able to penetrate the complexities of organizational folly and create an organization that works brilliantly.

Organizations follow *inescapable underlying structural principles* that are almost always unrecognized and therefore rarely addressed. In this book we are going to outline in detail the structural principles that organizations *must* follow in order for their destiny to be in their own hands.

Without an essential understanding of structure, managers – from the most senior positions – will be at the mercy of forces they cannot comprehend or influence. If we don't understand the underlying structure of the organization, *any* changes we attempt are bound to fail, including the soundest systems, the most enlightened policies, the most intelligent and advanced strategies, the most compelling vision, or the most sincerely held values.

Here's the point. *Structure is the most important and powerful influence there is within the organization. If we don't deal with structure, we won't be able to change the organization fundamentally.* With an understanding of structural principles we can *redesign* our organization so that change will finally succeed and our organization can evolve and prosper.

My use of the term *structure* at this point may seem abstract and vague, but we will define it, explore it, and work with it. Stay with me, and you'll come out the other side of this book amazed, disillusioned, and perhaps ready to take on a cause that will revolutionize the way organizations are designed in the future.

Most organizations are structured horribly. They are like Howard Hughes's aircraft 'The Spruce Goose'. They can get off the ground but the design is so bad that flight is barely manageable. Hughes took only one flight in his infamous aircraft. That single experience was enough to give him the wisdom never to attempt it again. There were better-designed planes in existence, so why waste time with one that was so poorly structured?

But for organizations the possibility of adopting a better-structured vehicle seems more limited. In the face of organizational absurdity most people eventually become philosophical: If the organizational 'spruce goose' is all we have, then let's fly it as best we can. That is all any of us can expect.

It's sad to see people spending thirty years of their lives in companies so poorly designed that their great collective energy and talents are wasted in repeated useless efforts at improvement – efforts which end with a rapid return to the same insipid situations.

Your organizational structures may be killing you. But right now, they are invisible to you.

Types of behaviour

Before we define structure let's talk about the types of behaviour structure produces. There are really only two types: *resolving* and *oscillating*.

Resolving behaviour describes moving *from somewhere* to *somewhere else*. When we throw a ball it moves *from our hand* to *where it lands*, from *one condition* to *another*.

In our organizations we want our actions to move us from *an actual state* (the current situation) to a *desired state* (our goals and aspirations) – movement that *resolves* once we achieve our ends.

The word *resolution* implies movement coming to an end. In our most effective organizations we see example after example of *resolving* behaviour. Action is first *generated* then *comes to an end* once a desired outcome is achieved. Project teams complete assignments, reports are written, budgets are prepared, advertising campaigns are carried out, goods are produced. Tens of thousands of repetitions of resolving behaviour are linked together when management of coordinates individual acts into an organizational tapestry of effective strategy.

Simultaneous and overlapping incidents of resolving behaviour reinforce each other beautifully, leading to an organizational state of alignment. When this is true, enormous feats are accomplished. When organizations are structured well, they produce networks of resolving behaviour which amplify the magnitude and scope of the enterprise. They have synergy. In such an organization each person's actions count and contribute to the energy and talent to the entire enterprise.

To anyone who has worked in a corporation this situation sounds utopian. Most organizations are not structured to bring out the best performance in their members or the company itself. Why? Because of the other type of behaviour a structure can produce is *oscillation*.

Oscillating behaviour acts exactly as it sounds. It moves from one place to another, *but then it moves back to its original position.*

To demonstrate the difference between resolving and oscillating behaviour for a roomful of managers I once used two of my daughter's toys: a small car and a doll's rocking chair. First, I pushed the rocking chair forward. When I took my hand off, it, of course, moved backwards. I repeated the demonstration a few times, and a predictable pattern of behaviour became obvious. Forward motion was followed by backward motion. Then I took the bright-red car and shot it down the middle of the aisle. It came to rest near the back of the room. The rocking chair is a good example of a structure that produces oscillating behaviour, the car an example of resolving behaviour.

Next I took the car and placed it on the seat of the rocking chair. 'This is like many organizations,' I explained as I moved the chair forwards then let it go. 'No matter how much resolving behaviour you have, the dominant structure still oscillates. In this type of organization, success eventually doesn't succeed.'

Then I placed the rocking chair on top of the car and pushed it down the aisle. 'This is like an organization in which a resolving structure is dominant, even if it happens to contain some oscillating behaviour. In this type of organization true progress can happen, and you can get where you want to go.'

Organizations want *resolving* behaviour but they are plagued with chronic *oscillating* behaviour. Just as in the movement of a rocking chair, once we move *towards* our goals we appear to reach a crucial point in which something seems to move us *away* from where we want to be. Every step forward seems to cause a step back, and progress is eventually neutralized.

Why did our success eventually lead to difficulties? Why did opportunities turn into problems? Everyone has a plausible explanation, but these explanations serve to cloud the real *structural* issue. Finger pointing may become a popular pastime as people attempt to decide why growth led to downsizing. Was it poor planning or bad leadership by senior management? Was it poor execution by the rank and file? Was it the economy? Competition from abroad? The cost of labour? Unimaginative research and development? A weak marketing strategy? Any or all of these factors might be present as *symptoms* but they are not the cause. The question of what *causes these symptoms* is rarely asked.

Success sometimes leads to failure

In an oscillating pattern individuals, teams, departments, and divisions may create success, but to what end? This is a car sitting in a rocking chair and spinning its wheels. *Success in one department can even cause difficulties in other parts of the organization.* Increased sales can strain manufacturing capacity. New products can confuse buyers and lead to instability in established markets. Reinvestment in manufacturing facilities can lead to declining stock market performance.

The relationship of the parts to the whole is not obvious because organizations are fragmented by a division of labour. Department heads are focused on their own local interests, which are usually the accomplishment of their goals. Inadvertently, conflicts of interest develop between competing forces – engineering versus marketing, finance versus strategic planning, marketing versus sales, R&D versus operations, and so on.

Are engineers, for example, the natural enemy of the marketing department? The way many organizations are structured it would seem so. Usually, there is a conflict between what the engineers want and what the marketing people want. The engineers want to make the best-designed product they can and the marketing people want to get a new product into the hands of the customer as quickly as possible, giving the company a competitive advantage. The conflict is the classic *quality* versus *timeliness*.

Since these two groups have competing mandates within the organization the best that we could hope for is a cold war type of balance of power in which neither side wins or loses. What a waste of organizational energy as both sides work against the aims of the other and against the ultimate aim of the organization.

Oscillating behaviour in a rocking chair is a wonderful thing, given what we want it to do, which is rock back and forth. But in an organization oscillating behaviour works against the aims of the enterprise.

It's hard to see what's going on

One reason it is hard to see what is really going on is that oscillating movement can take a long period of time, even years. When oscillation moves that slowly it is not obvious that a structural pattern is in play unless we know how to understand long-range patterns. The shorter time-frame is filled with immediate events which seem to call for reactions or responses, our focus is drawn to the immediate demands of the circumstances. This isn't wrong. When difficulties dominate the scene the most natural human instinct is to address them. But if we address only symptoms we become distracted from their causes and true change on the causal structural level becomes unlikely. If problem solving and crisis intervention becomes the chronic managerial process long-range building becomes unlikely. We think that if we take corrective action we have solved the problem. But the flurry of activity hides what is really going on. We are deceived by a temporary fix. Later, the same type of problem reoccurs or a new problem arises out of the ashes of a previous solution – one that we thought was completely successful.

Another reason that oscillating patterns of behaviour are hard to see is that at least half the time the organization is moving in the direction it wants to go. Progress seems like it's been achieved and everyone congratulates each other. Nevertheless, in such a pattern, *because* of the success, difficulties are bound to happen. *In an oscillating pattern movement in one direction will* **precipitate** *eventual movement in the other.*

In an oscillating pattern our success can fool us and our eventual difficulties surprise us. For the IBMs, the GMs, and the DECs of the world, success seemed to be unending during their growth periods. How were they to know that they were subject to oscillation? When the cycle changed, profits declined and markets weakened, those in senior positions were vilified, as if they caused the problems. Did they? Or were they also the victims of an oscillating structure in which past success was bound to lead to future decline? Even leaders can be victims of an inadequate structure.

These trends could have been predicted and prevented *if the people involved in those organizations understood the inherent structures in play.*

Leadership

Here is a point that my friend and colleague Peter Senge has often made. We often think of a leader as captain of the ship, commander of the troops, the person in charge of big decisions. Filled with vision for the future, energy to meet the challenge, and personal magnetism to engage the masses, he or she forges distinct and divergent parts into a well-conceived whole. But there is another image of leadership that has less sex appeal and less of a mythical tradition, but is just as compelling. That is the leader as architect and designer. Who has more real influence, after all? The captain of the ship or the ship's designer? In *Star Trek* we love Captain Kirk as he uses his cunning to defeat the Romulins. But he is subject to the design of the *Enterprise* as is everyone else aboard the starship. The cause of dramatic interest would not be served by an episode in which a group of engineers sit around a room and quietly design a starship. Yet the truth is that no matter how imaginative and courageous the captain is, he or she is always subject to the ship's structure and must act accordingly.

Leadership does require a captain, of course. Decisions need to be made, the course set, and the crew instructed. But the best leaders are also involved with elements of design. A leader who thinks structurally can determine the desired outcomes *and* the design of the vehicle used to achieve the vision. The organization is not unlike a ship. It is a vehicle conceived for transport. It seeks to travel from point to point through time and space – from smaller to larger markets, from simple businesses to more complex ones, from local to world-wide engagement. Is it any wonder that the organization that works like a rocking chair works against everyone's aspirations?

But organizations have a distinct advantage over ships. They can be redesigned en route to their destination. Sometimes small changes are all that is necessary to move an organization from an oscillating pattern of behaviour to a resolving one. Sometimes a major overhaul is needed to accomplish an essential structural change. But when change is occurring on the level of structure, the desired outcomes can be accomplished.

What is structure?

Structure describes how the *parts* of anything *relate* to each other and to the whole. Take a director's chair, for example. It has two sets of lets, two arms, a back and a seat. By themselves these are simply independent elements. They do not make up a structure. If these parts were not connected each would fall to the ground. But within the structure of the chair they are *connected.*

The connection affects the movement of each part by limiting the degree to which each can fall. The legs prevent the seat from falling and the seat, arms, and back from falling. Each part influences the behaviour of the other. Stability is formed by the *relationship* of each part to the other.

In business many people use the term *structure* to describe a simple reporting relationship. Joe and Sally report to Harry, who, in turn, reports to Mary, who reports to Sam, etc. The relationships described do not tell us anything about the *influence* the relationships have on each other. The use of the term *structure* here is misleading. For simple reporting relationships do not tell us anything about how parts influence each other and the whole.

Not all relationships are structural, such as a loose association of elements that do not affect each other. Aggregations of items, such as a stamp collection, a butterfly collection, a social club, or a shelf of various books are often simply an assortment of elements that do not, by virtue of their association, generate specific tendencies for behaviour as do structural relationships.

For a relationship to be structural, *the elements must be connected, and the connection must affect each of the elements which are connected.* Structural relationships lead to tendencies for behaviour.

In the case of our director's chair, the parts by themselves cannot function as a chair. Only when they are connected to each other do they form a whole, creating a tendency for stability.

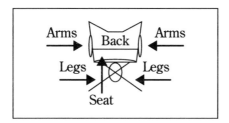

When we think about organizations we usually think about the parts as parts and not as *relationships* between the parts. In order to understand why organizations behave the ways they do, however, we must see how these parts are linked, and the structure that they create. In the next chapter we will begin to explore the nature of structure and how structure creates tendencies for behaviour.

2 The tension-resolution system

The basic units of mathematics are *numbers*. The basic units of language are *words*. The basic units of structure are *tension-resolution systems*. A tension is formed by the *discrepancy* between something and something else. A tension-resolution system results from the fact that whenever there is a tension it will strive for resolution.

Unless we have discrepancy we don't have a tension. And if we don't have a tension, we don't have a structure, in the same way that if we didn't have numbers, we wouldn't have mathematics, or if we didn't have words, we wouldn't have language.

A simple example of a tension is thirst. There is a discrepancy between how much liquid the body needs and how much it actually has. This discrepancy creates a tension, which, in turn, produces a *tendency for movement – towards* action that ends the discrepancy. Thirst is resolved by drinking liquid until the body's desired state is the same as the body's actual state:

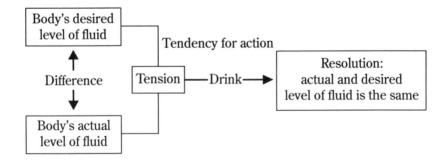

In this simple example we can observe some of the most important principles about structure:

1 Tension is formed by a *discrepancy* between two elements.
2 Tension creates a *tendency for movement.*
3 Tension resolves *when the discrepancy ends.*

If we want to create an outcome *we can form a tension that will move in that direction, and resolve once the outcome is achieved.* This principle is enormously important for organizations which are in the business of creating desired outcomes.

Structural tension

It is important to know that we can *create* structural relationships by orchestrating tension. Once we form a tension, we set up tendencies for movement. Like an archer with a bow and arrow poised to hit the target, the *tension* leads to an impetus for *action* which leads to *resolution* of the tension.

How do we form the kind of tension that is particularly useful to the organization? First, we need to know what *result* we want. What is the outcome? Where do we want the tension to resolve? What is the target?

This sounds simple enough, but I have found that most people do not know what they want. I have worked with many management teams who *thought* they knew what they were after. But once we began to have a discussion on that subject it turned out that they had very different ideas from each other.

When it comes to identifying the results they want people are often vague. Or they think only in terms of solutions to problems – the elimination of what they *don't* want. Or they limit their thinking to what seems possible within the situation, and therefore censor themselves from thinking about their broader desires. Later, we will develop the theme of *end results* in more detail so you will be able to advance your ability to conceive the outcomes you actually want. For now, it is enough to say that *step one* in forming a tension is to begin with what you want to create – the desired state.

The next step is to identify the actual state that currently exists. This also sounds simple. But people are in the habit of distorting reality, especially in organizations. An accurate evaluation of the current reality is clouded by a mixture of theories, speculations, propaganda, defensive posturing, and a general lack of discipline.

Fact and 'other than fact' are confused until 'other than fact' can seem like objective fact.

In many organizations telling it like it truly is can be dangerous. For example, one company with which I have consulted had a 'value statement' that included *honesty* on the list. But people within the organization reported that the reality was quite different. Individuals would regularly misrepresent the truth when faced with failure. 'No one ever admits failure in this company,' one senior vice president told me. 'If someone fails, it is always reported as a success. Telling the truth is hazardous within this company's political climate. People are promoted for playing the system, and the system encourages us to lie through our teeth.'

Organizations in which people habitually misrepresent the truth are severely dysfunctional. It is hard to get the facts we need, evaluate success or failure, make advantageous decisions, build adroit strategies, or improve, learn, and develop. An organization in which people are objective and accurate about reality has a distinct competitive advantage because quick adjustment can be made, learning can occur, and the course corrected as needed. Furthermore, if the organization knows where it wants to go, accomplishing *step two* in forming tension is easy and useful.

Once we have identified what we want (the desired state) and what we currently have relative to our desired outcome (the actual state) we have created *structural tension*.[1] Often, we form structural tension

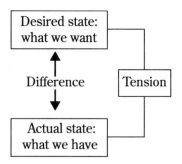

---

1 *Structural tension* is the term I have given to this particular structural relationship. Some who have adopted my work have called this 'creative tension'. The term 'creative' is misleading, because *creative* means departure from the norm. If anything, we would want this structure to become the norm in our organizations. Since I invented and first named this concept, I prefer people to call it structural tension, which properly emphasizes the *structural* nature of the relationship.

unconsciously and instinctively. Another way of describing it is haphazardly and inadvertently. When we consciously form structural tension we are more able to manage the processes we use, the actions we take, the course corrections we make, and the momentum we produce.

Several of my clients are now using the principle of structural tension as the basis for their strategic planning. End results are accurately and precisely identified and current reality rigorously reported.

Let me describe some of the types of changes that *naturally* occur as a consequence of this process. People are very clear about the results they are working towards, and because of this clarity, they keep their collective focus on the same point. This is a different situation from what we find in many organizations where people have simply memorized a set of phrases that have been publicized throughout the company. When asked what the statements mean, each person has a different answer and a different understanding.

Instead of giving superficial lip service to company proclamations people who use structural tension have a depth of understanding about where the organization wants to go. As current reality changes, managers are able to track the changes and accurately report them to each other. Gone are the bad habits of excessive speculation about what might be going on, the theorizing about how things should have turned out, the finger pointing and blaming, the distorting of reality for self-serving ends, and the political positioning. When people use their desired end results as the basis for their collective efforts they are suddenly in the same boat going in the same direction. Furthermore, when they do have different perceptions about what is going on, rather than fight it out as to who is right and who is wrong, they all want to know what reality truly is and why they might see it differently.

Instead of blaming each other for actions that didn't work they enter into a collective-learning process in which mistakes *and* successes are vehicles for learning and improvement. They objectively evaluate the actions they have taken and are open to finding out exactly what is going on. This new openness is another inherent side-effect of using structural tension as the common organizing principle.

An organization we worked with created a high-tech system that connects all computers of various platforms from personal to mainframe. Their customers included many *Fortune 500* companies and each installation cost between $50 000 and as much as $200 000. The company was originally driven by brilliant engineering; the direction the business took was determined by their state-of-the-art product, in the early days of the company the most advanced in the market. When we first started asking members of the organization about their goals the engineers said that they liked solving technical problems; the product developers said they wanted to correct problems with the current offering; the marketing department said they wanted to sell their product to anyone they could, and management said they were trying to keep everybody happy. They all had developed goals, but no one believed the goals were important. In some areas they were understaffed, in others overstaffed. The organization was always reacting to the growing complexities of the business and responding to customers' demands. So everyone's time was filled with problem solving and incremental improvement of the product.

The managers were bogged down in day-to-day affairs and no one was taking the future very seriously. One reason for this was their history. They had developed their business without much planning or forethought. The company was successful because, at that point, they had very little competition, a situation that was about to change.

We had a meeting with the senior management, all the department heads, and all other key players and put this simple question to them: *'What do you want?'*

At first they were vague and defensive. Some of the managers thought they had enough on their plate and didn't want to add any more work. Others had never before thought in terms of desired end results. Instead, they had organized themselves around the prevailing problems that were currently demanding their attention.

The first few hours was a distinctly unpleasant experience for all of us. The walls were papered with flipchart sheets that demonstrated the inner workings of their organizational mind, which turned out to be chaotic, contradictory, defensive, and combative. The next few hours were spent in sorting out what they wanted for their company in the future – a 'What do you want to be when you grow up?' kind of thing.

Before we prepare to form goals we need to know how the company works as a business. How does it generate revenues? In this case, the company developed and distributed high-tech products that required ongoing research and development to accommodate the changes in computer platforms. The process of developing desired end results therefore needed to include goals that supported their R&D capacity, their understanding of the latest computer technology, and how they could tie their efforts to marketplace needs.

To refine the process we made a distinction between items on their list that were designed to fix problems – the elimination of what was *unwanted – and* true end results – what they really wanted to see exist. For the sake of the exercise they were asked to separate what they thought was possible from what they actually wanted, because many of them refused to say what they wanted if it didn't seem possible. Little by little, the real desired end results began to appear.

As soon as these few end results were written down the energy in the room changed dramatically. It was as if the group went from driving an old car with the brakes dragging to driving a finely tuned high-performance sports car. This exercise was not a brainstorming session in which people were free-associating – a practice that is incapable of leading to genuine strategic thinking. Instead, it was focused, rigorous, and filled with astute critical thinking.

At the end of the first stage the organization had identified eight company-wide end results that were tied to their business strategy. In tandem, these end results created a unity of intent and direction. Each end result reinforced the other end results, and each added flesh to the skeleton of the business strategy.

We then identified the current reality of each result. The discussion about current reality went quickly and smoothly, because the end results had given the group a lens through which to view reality clearly. Next, we created strategies to enable the organization to accomplish its goals.

One of their goals was to acquire a share of the international market. The strategy they devised was to be acquired by a major multinational corporation that could better support their entry into the international arena. The current reality was they were not an attractive proposition for acquisition at that time.

Over the next few years the organization managed itself by the principles of structural tension, grew, and prospered. Its 'shotgun' approach to management (do as much as we can and hope we hit a few targets) was reorganized into a refined targeted strategy. Eventually, the company was acquired by a multinational corporation. The shareholders received a nice profit from the sale and the organization was in a strong position to enter world markets with new products.

All the organizations we work with adopt the practice of using structural tension for the basis of their management strategy. What we have found is that the more difficult the type of managerial complexity, the more that structural tension charting is needed as an organizing process. It is not uncommon for an ambitious project to require over a hundred interconnected structural tension charts which allow a high degree of control over the activities of the group without resorting to micro-management.

Tendencies for movement

When we were infants most of our world was arranged into a series of *instinctive* tension-resolution systems. When we were tired we slept. When we were hungry, we cried to be fed. But why did we get hungry? Because there was a discrepancy between the amount of food our bodies required and the actual amount of food we actually had. Hunger is a tension that leads to action – eating – designed to end the discrepancy. The tension is resolved when the actual amount of food is the same as the amount of food the body needs to sustain itself.

As we grow and mature we move from *instinctive* to *self-conceived* tension-resolution systems. Infants want immediate gratification. We learn how to delay resolution in favour of outcomes that we desire. Instead of spending every penny we have as quickly as we can, we begin to save our money for more costly purchase. We begin to plan ahead and increase our ability to create what matters to us.

As an organization matures it too can develop a greater ability to use self-conceived rather than instinctive tension-resolution systems. Rather than simply reacting to the latest crisis, it is able to orchestrate its own long-term strategies by forming and managing structural tension.

Structural tension is a *generative* structure. Its very nature leads to action. Without it, we would have to manipulate ourselves into action. Our efforts would be forced and would eventually run out of steam. But when we create structural tension the natural inclination is action. It is more natural to act in favour of our desired outcomes than to do nothing.

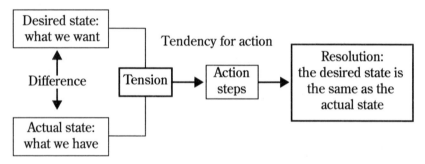

The principle of structural tension can be universally applied throughout the organization. Every aspect of the company can benefit from organizing itself into units of structural tension. At the most general level this involves the most important governing ideas of the organization – its purpose, mission, vision, and values – in other words, its reason to exist. These governing ideas have a desired end result (the fulfilment of the aspirations) and a current reality (the actual level of accomplishment). At the local level, desired end results can be accurately identified and placed in the context of the current reality. Furthermore, managerial coordination between departments and divisions becomes more likely when the desired outcomes are clear and the current reality is continually evaluated.

I suppose this sounds like simple common sense. 'If you know what you want and know what you have, then it is easy to move from where you are to where you want to be.' But let me caution you. Many organizations think they are doing what I am describing, but they are not. They think they have identified their desired outcomes because they have goals. But when we look at these goals we usually find a mishmash of ingredients that do not fit together, particularly when we attempt to match one department's goal with those of other departments. Later in this book we will go into how to conceptualize and formulate desired outcomes for the entire company. For now, it is enough to say that goal setting in many organizations is a severely flawed process.

If we haven't identified the end results we want we are unable to identify that part of the current reality that is specific to our desired outcomes. With all the information that is available in today's world of supercomputers it can be hard to judge what is relevant and what is not. If we are unable to use our desired end results as a guide we would have to examine *all* information as if it were of equal importance. We would soon become overwhelmed, and the chances of understanding reality would decrease, even as we study the information more. Not all information is of equal importance, but without a standard of measurement rooted in focused outcomes it is hard to know what to analyse and what to file.

Most organizations seem to have a distinct aversion to reality. Partly this is due to a general lack of experience in objectively reporting reality – the news, rather than the editorial. But another part is structural. Many organizations have structured into their management reward systems conflicts which encourage people to distort reality. This is a theme we will develop later in this book, as we will show *how to use the principle of structural tension as a strategic planning tool, a management and leadership skill, and an instrument for organizing the entire enterprise*. But before we take on such an ambitious task we need to know more about structure.

As we said, structure produces *two* types of behaviour – resolving and oscillating. Structural tension produces resolving behaviour, and if all you got out of this book was a knowledge of how to create structural tension you would be faring very well indeed. However, you would not be able to understand or change what is going on when an oscillating structure is in play.

Oscillating patterns

Most organizations have many patterns of oscillation which recycle regularly. Decision making can move from tightly centralized control in which very few people in senior management positions make all the major decisions to decentralized control, in which many people from various segments of the organization are given the responsibility to make major decisions. During good times decision making tends to be decentralized, but when economic times become difficult many fear that decisions are not well coordinated. When a crisis hits, those in senior positions usually reclaim their authority.

Another related recurring cycle involves independence. Members of the organization are first encouraged to take independent action and then are required to march in close step with their management teams. The financial direction of the organization can move from an emphasis on cost-cutting, to investment, back to cost-cutting. The company as a whole can move from an inventive mode, to an emphasis on convention, back to innovation. Organizations expand, then downsize, then expand once again. In these types of oscillating patterns the organization loses money, time, resources, intellectual capital, morale, reputation, and market share.

No one wants these oscillating patterns, so why do they exist? They exist because of another fundamental structural mechanism I call *structural conflict*.

Structural conflict

While structural tension is produced by a *simple* tension-resolution system *structural conflict* results from a more complex structural arrangement. It is the product of two tension-resolution systems.

A simple non-organizational example will allow us to see how a structural conflict produces the kind of wasteful and demoralizing oscillating behaviour that undermines most organizations. Hunger produces a tension that is resolved by eating.

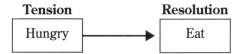

But if we are overweight, and diet, we are subject to another tension-resolution system:

As each system moves towards its own resolution it competes with the conflicting system. First, the dominant tension is hunger. In order to resolve that tension we eat:

Once we have eaten, our hunger subsides but our weight goes up. The amount we weigh is discrepant with the amount we want to weigh. This discrepancy becomes the more pronounced tension:

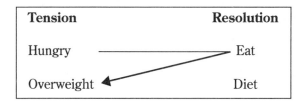

In order to resolve this tension, we eat less or skip meals:

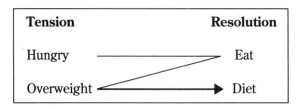

We may lose some pounds and we begin to feel better about our weight. But the body reacts to the reduction of fat and protein. It sends a life-and-death starvation warning by triggering the brain's appestat, which in turn, encourages the body to store a higher percentage of fat than usual, and also to increase the appetite in order to store even more fat. The discrepancy between the body's desired amount of food and the actual amount of food increases even more than it was before the diet. Hunger, once again, becomes the bigger tension as the brain relays the message – 'Eat! Eat! Eat!'

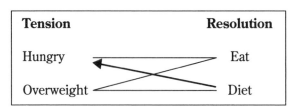

The shift of dominance between the first and second tension-resolution systems produces a predictable pattern of behaviour. Hunger leads to eating which leads to weight gain, which leads to dieting, which leads to hunger.

The movement from the first tension-resolution system to the second produces an oscillating *behaviour* that is familiar to anyone who has tried dieting – but failed. Yet the *structure* causing the failure is not obvious. People who experience this cycle fear they are to blame for being weak-willed or lacking discipline. They do not realize that, within this structure, no amount of heightened resolve will work. Every time they force themselves into a diet the structure compensates for the movement and, eventually, their best efforts fail. They are up against a structure that is inadequate for the resolving behaviour they desire. As with a rocking chair, any movement forwards is followed by a movement backwards. That is all the structure can do as one tension-resolution system shifts to the other, then back again.

The change–continuity conflict

We have asked why change within the organization is difficult, and the answer is that structural conflicts lead to oscillating behaviours. In the following example an organization is trapped in a structural conflict that causes it to first embrace then reject change.

The organization wants change in order to improve its performance, avoid stagnation, and capitalize on its potential. It institutes a programme and changes begin to occur. Systems are reorganized, cross-discipline teams are formed, new evaluation methods are adopted, people move to new positions, and so on:

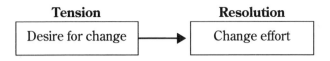

Tension   **Resolution**

| Desire for change | → | Change effort |

But as the changes take place they bring with them a degree of instability and discontinuity. Work becomes harder to accomplish as familiar lines of communication disappear. People begin to feel unsure of what is expected of them, of what they need to do to fulfil the new mandates, and of who is now in charge. Even though the new policies and principles are clearly stated, the actual conditions seem quite different from the ideals being expressed. In the light of all the upheaval people begin to long for continuity, and eventually this becomes a dominant tension:

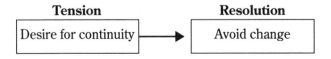

Tension   **Resolution**

| Desire for continuity | → | Avoid change |

This tension is resolved by rejecting change. People may bypass the new lines of authority or ignore new policies. Support for the changes weakens as factions develop. The change effort becomes subtly undermined and morale dips.

At this point in the cycle the organization has returned to business as usual and the change effort is recognized as a failure. But a return to the old ways brings its own set of problems. Growth is limited, creativity restrained, and improvement stifled. After a time of living with stagnation new calls for change fill the air.

Over periods of years the company cycles through several shifts of *change* to *continuity*. Each change effort grows out of limitation and stagnation; each move back to the status quo comes from the discontinuity that the change efforts have brought.

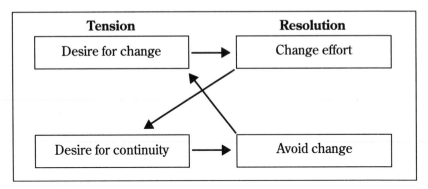

Many organizations are subject to this structure without understanding all the dynamics in play. Change is resisted, but so is stagnation. Continuity and change seem in a constant, unwinnable battle with each other. The experience people often have is that of neither losing nor gaining ground. Or perhaps every new change effort (for even the simplest advancements) requires mounting an enormous campaign. After a while members of the organization may begin to wonder if change is worth the trouble.

Let's look more closely at the actual causes of these types of shifts. Imagine a rubber band – a tension-resolution system – tied around us as we move towards our first desired state: *change*:

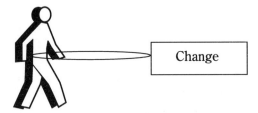

Now imagine another rubber band, tied around us, but connected to our other desired state: *continuity*:

As we move toward the first of our goals – change – that tension-resolution system begins to resolve. But what is happening to the other tension-resolution system, to the rubber band connected to *continuity*? It is stretching, and the tension in that system is increasing.

Now where is it easier for us to move? Where is the path of least resistance? Obviously, away from our goal of change and towards our goal of continuity.

But as soon as the *continuity* rubber band begins to resolve, the *change* rubber band begins to stretch. Its tension is increasing. Where is it now easier for us to move? Back towards change – again.

The oscillation between the theme of change and the theme of continuity repeats itself again and again. When change is addressed, the desire for continuity gradually increases until it becomes the dominant theme. People act to restore the organization's sense of continuity. But the pendulum shifts yet again, and people begin to hope for change to support growth and expansion of the enterprise.

The shifts may take years – so slowly that it is hard to observe that a *predictable pattern* is in play. Other issues appear on the scene and demand attention, and events seem to rise out of the immediate situation. However, the real cause of the conditions will not be found in the personnel but in the structure which is inadequate for *change, growth,* or *continuity.*

What does the structure want?

This next point is important if we are to understand why structural conflict operates the way it does. Let us pose this question: What does the structure want? In other words, what is the structure's goal?

The situation is this. Two tension-resolution systems are competing against each other. Each individual system has the local structural goal of resolving that system's tension. But it is impossible to resolve both systems simultaneously because whenever we move towards resolution in one system the tension in the other intensifies. The shift of dominance from one system to the other produces the tendency to oscillation. The structure cannot resolve both tension-resolution systems simultaneously because of the imbalance that exists between them. Here is a key factor: *imbalance.* The structure wants to reduce the *imbalance,* to create a *balance* or *equilibrium* between the two tension-resolution systems.

When I say the structure 'wants' balance I do not mean to imply that structure has a mind, a will of its own, a personality, or a vested interest in the outcome, any more than gravity has. It is an impersonal fact of nature.

The structure wants *equilibrium,* but we want something that will produce *non-equilibrium.* We may want change:

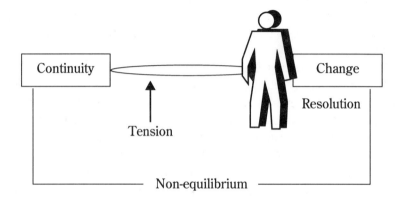

or continuity:

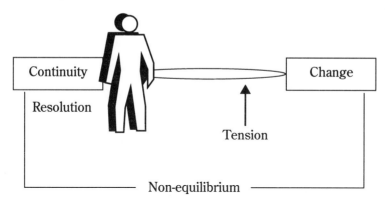

But the structure wants balance between the two competing tension-resolution systems, so that each tension equals the other:

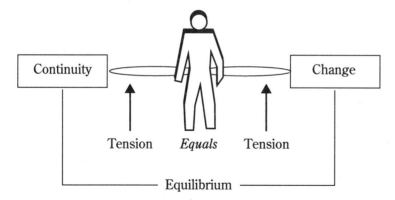

Within this structural conflict any time we move towards *change,* equilibrium is lost. If we move towards *continuity,* it is also lost. Movement towards either side of the conflict sets up an imbalance. The structure tends to compensate for imbalance by moving towards equilibrium.

When we understand the structural dynamics in play we are less likely to take sides, be it on the side of change or of continuity. We know that movement in either direction only serves to widen the magnitude of the oscillation, and create a tendency to move in the other direction in order to compensate for the imbalance. But neither do we want to be stuck between change and continuity. Structural conflict, as we can see, is an inadequate structure in which to accomplish our purpose – successful change while maintaining adequate continuity.

Structural conflicts are not problems

Structural conflicts are not problems. They are simply inadequate structures to accomplish our ends. They are like rocking chairs, structures that are designed to oscillate. That's all they can do. If we found ourselves in a rocking chair but we wanted to travel to town we would not attempt to 'fix' our rocking chair by putting wheels on it, or installing a motor, steering wheel and brakes. We would move from the rocking chair to a car.

The analogy holds true for organizations. When we are confronted with inadequate structures our temptation is to enter into a problem-solving mode rather than abandon that structure for a more useful one. But once we have identified a structural conflict, such as the change–continuity one, it is possible to form a new and more useful structure to enable us to create what we want. Here is the principle:

Rather than attempting to fix an inadequate structure, establish a more suitable one.

We have been taught that when something is wrong, fix it. But fixing something that is ill-designed to begin with does little to help us achieve our aims. In Chapter 4 we will address a more useful approach to organizational predicaments, redesigning the essential structures that drive the behaviours. Before we consider organizational redesign, however, in the next chapter we will delve into some of the most prevalent structural conflicts found in today's organizations.

3   Structural conflicts

In this chapter we are going to describe some of the major structural conflicts that managers must contend with throughout their organizational lives. Our discussion is not meant to be a formulaic approach to the structural phenomenon. We do not want simply to prescribe solutions or promote various types of behaviour. *Rather, we want to develop an understanding of how these types of conflicts evolve, so that we can increase our ability to think structurally – in other words, to think in terms of the relationships that lead to oscillating behaviour.* This will enable us to identify other structural conflicts that may exist, in addition to the ones that are mentioned here.

Growth and limitation

Organizations are in the business of expanding their operation in many areas – their markets, their profits, their product mix, their customer service, their scale, their scope, and so on. Most managers rightfully see the general growth of the company as one of their major responsibilities. So why do many organizations experience critical limitations when they attempt to expand the company? The answer lies in a structural conflict between *growth* and *capacity*. The *desire to expand* is resolved by *growth*.

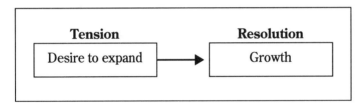

But as we grow, we stress the organization's *capacity*. Growth increases the workload, which will lead to:

• The same amount of people doing more work or
• New people added.

If the same number of people are doing more work they become less efficient. Management may hope to reorganize the way people work so that greater productivity will come from the same number of people. Usually this idea looks good on paper but fails in reality. The increased workload often does not lead to new and inventive procedures for two reasons. First, the worst time to ask people to adopt new methods is when they are feeling overwhelmed. Second, there is a learning curve associated with adopting new methods: people are always *less* efficient before they learn to be *more* efficient. Faced with increasing demands, their tendency will be to relapse into familiar, 'tried and true' work habits rather than taking on new and unfamiliar methods.

If we take on more people to do the extra work the workload will not decrease at once because the new people need to be trained. Who will train them? The very people whose workload has just increased. New people will *add* to the strain on capacity before they are able to reduce the workload.

A similar phenomenon occurs when new technology is added to increase productivity of the existing workforce. The learning curve needed to master the new systems strains capacity temporarily before it is of any real help.

Those measures that are designed to increase capacity come up against *the current level of capacity which can seem fixed*. This produces a strain on capacity, leading to a shift in dominance by a second tension-resolution system. The tension that drives the second tension-resolution system is the discrepancy between the *actual capacity* of the organization and the *amount of capacity that is demanded* by the growth that has taken place.

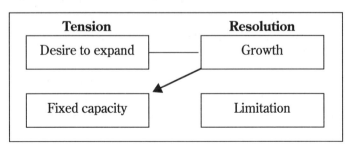

The more growth there is, the more capacity is strained. Fixed capacity becomes the dominant system, and resolves itself by limiting the growth.

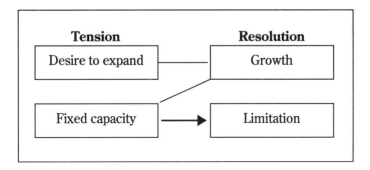

Once growth is limited, the strain on capacity decreases, and everyone breathes a little easier for a while. But once the relationship between capacity and limitation becomes less discrepant, the desire to grow once again is the dominant theme.

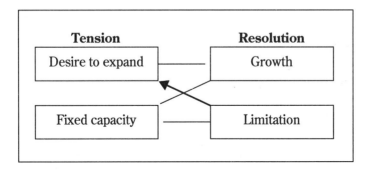

The following is a common pattern in organizations:

- Start out on a course aimed at growth.
- As the volume of the company's activities increases, capacity becomes strained.
- Growth slows down as people shift their attention to managing capacity issues.

Usually capacity is not fixed, but it takes a longer time-frame to increase capacity than it does to expand in other ways. The lag time, itself, functions as if capacity were fixed, or at least fixed at a rate that is too slow for the desired rate of expansion.

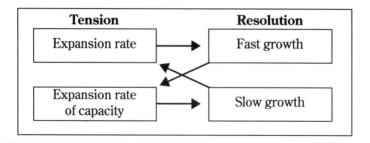

The relationship between capacity and growth is a vital element in the overall success of the organization's expansion goals, but often the organization's management of this relationship is haphazardly conceived. Many companies neglect important questions of capacity through an informal generalized policy of 'Let's minimize our cost of doing business'. In some organizations workloads are strained to the point at which only the workaholics can survive in the stress-filled environment. Everyone is so busy that they do not have time to reflect on the *way* they work. Therefore they are unlikely to invent new methods that would be more efficient and effective. They may want to change the situation and they may even hire consultants who offer useful advice. But they're unable to take the advice because they're just too busy. 'This is our culture' people proclaim almost proudly, as if there were something destined about their chronic overload. In such an organization attempts to grow and expand are met with great resistance, because the last thing people want is more work.

In some organizations senior management delivers two often conflicting messages: 'Meet your growth goals and minimize your expenses'. In the following structural conflict we will see a shift of dominance from the themes of strained workload to those of budgetary concerns resulting in expanding then downsizing only a few years later. A few years after that, more people are added once again to meet the pressures of the understaffed organization.

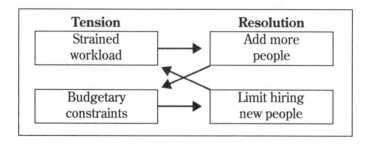

Another, related, structural conflict which makes a comprehensive strategy of balancing growth and capacity unlikely occurs when profit goals are in contention with the desire to expand capacity. The debate is between the financial people who are trained to think in terms of limiting costs and the managers who think in terms of accomplishing the work of the company.

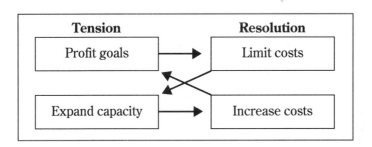

Building a business calls for investment and development over a period of many years, and so the business person's focus is usually on long-range development. Financial people, on the other hand, think in shorter time-frames. Because they are able to produce a more immediate impact on the bottom line by cost-cutting measures their focus naturally gravitates towards managing costs. Financial types became very influential in many companies during the 1980s. Through their efforts, many corporations began to manage their profitability by manipulating financial factors such as stock trades, investment strategies, and so on. The dominance of financially based strategies proved to be short-sighted indeed, as many companies fell behind global competitors who were investing in their own growth and development.

Longer-range business strategies designed to expand the business are based on a different premise from financial manipulations. The premise is that in order to build the business and increase profitability, the organization must increase its ability to *generate* new business. Financial people tend to be focused on investing the money that is coming into the company; business people are focused on getting money to come into the company in the first place, as well as investing in the future growth of the enterprise. A business-oriented manager would authorize funds dedicated to long-term goals, which may appear to the financially oriented managers as an unjustifiable expense. Even such essential matters as training to expand the capacity of the workforce can be influenced by the conflict between competing *profit* versus *capacity* goals.

Mark W. Snowberger, once a finance executive and now president of Gilbarco North America, knows this conflict intimately. 'If you take someone off the floor [for training purposes]', he told *Industry Week* magazine, 'they're not making product. That gives rise to variance [a negative figure on the manufacturing profit and loss statement].... Therefore, the prevailing philosophy among manufacturing managers is "I can't afford to train my people or I'll wind up with negative variances". And then some accountant is going to say, "Look at how much money you cost the company".' While many of the investments necessary for the long-term growth of a company can look like black holes to a financial manager, as Mr Snowberger pointed out, spending money on things like training are just part of the cost of doing business.

From a business perspective like Mr Snowberger's, investing in increased capacity is included in the cost of doing business – a requirement. But to the financially oriented manager this cost is a needless expense. In a structural conflict, these two points of view are more than a philosophical disagreement. The structural conflict leads to oscillations between times when the pressure is on to turn in a good financial performance and times when expanding capacity is deemed necessary to stay competitive in the marketplace. As the oscillation shifts direction, one and then the other point of view become the basis for determining policy and strategy.

The following, similar structural conflict has led many organizations to an oscillating pattern of interrupted business expansion and inconsistent profit configurations as major corporate decisions shifted in direction from a business to a financial focus over time.

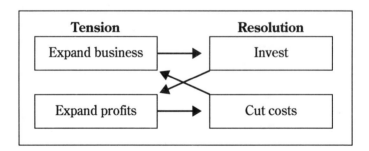

Wall Street has a lot to answer for when it comes to the economic fate many corporations have suffered in recent years. In the past, people who invested in stock usually tried to pick well-respected companies; and then hold the stock for many years, perhaps even passing it to their children. Holding stock helped the company to invest in their long-term future, and investment in stock was supportive of the long-range benefits of both company and stockholder. But that type of thinking has radically changed in the past number of decades. A gambler's fever now afflicts many investors. This has led to a devastating structural conflict that forces those in senior management positions to make decisions that are not in the best interests of the company.

What do investors in stock want? High return on investment.

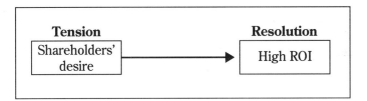

What does the organization want? Capital to invest in the development of the enterprise. But when capital is used for reinvestment, immediate profitability goes down, and the money available for shareholders' dividends is reduced until the investment can be recouped by growth.

A conflict of interest develops between the shareholders and the organization and produces oscillation:

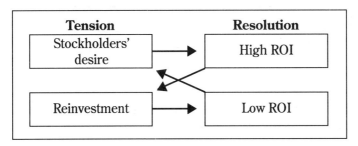

The focus within the organization is on building additional capacity. New plants are built, or new technology developed, costing money and time. No one knows for certain if these additions will increase the fortunes of the company, and, as the investment is implemented the performance of the stock begins to fall. The immediate attractiveness of the stock declines based on the company's unpredictable future.

The stock performance affects the organization's cost of capital. Money becomes more expensive. Other companies, whose stock is performing better in the market, can borrow money at lower interest rates and therefore enjoy a competitive advantage. The company begins to look vulnerable, and images of hostile take-overs loom on the horizon. A crisis develops, and senior management is asked to focus on the performance of the stock. The organization reconsiders its position, and begins to work toward making the stock more attractive to the marketplace. The focus shifts from reinvestment to stock performance – from business development to financial management.

Today, those who invest in stock achieve their major return on investment when the stock is sold – not held. Stockbrokers make money by trading stocks, so they are interested in more transactions, not fewer. This makes the short-term performance of the stock more important to the investors than the long-term viability of the company. As the company attempts to invest in its long-term future, short-term demands begin to dominate. Then as the company loses its competitiveness, longer-term strategies are developed once again. This structural conflict will produce shifts in managerial focus over several years, and lead the organization to instability.

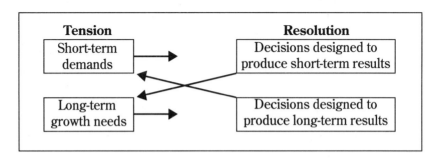

Let's look at this structural phenomenon from the perspective of our rubber band analogy. As we move towards our long-term goals, short-term demands increase the tension on the opposing rubber band. Where is it easier for us to go? In the direction of addressing short-term demands that seem to require our immediate attention.

We begin to study the issues that call for our immediate attention. But as we do, the need to concentrate on our longer-term strategies once again demands our consideration. Now, where is it easier for us to go? Back to questions of long-term strategy.

This structural conflict produces fluctuation in leadership and direction. It seems as if the organization can't make up its mind. Does it want to develop its long-range plans of reinvesting in the company, or is it in the business of selling stock? Senior management's oscillating behaviour between these two points can lead to appalling decisions that undermine morale and organizational alignment.

Many Western corporations have fallen victim to this structure as companies have merged, been acquired, changed management, changed direction, and even changed industries. This structure is less dominant in Asia, particularly in the large Japanese companies. Why? Because long-term planning produces *structural tension* as the organizing principle, and conflicts of interests are managed within that frame. The entire organization is governed with its eye on its desired end results. As reality changes, it is well studied and tactics are adjusted accordingly.

Some Japanese companies have created 200-year strategic plans. Many Western managers scoff at what seems to them an excessive exercise in charting the unknown. They argue that many of the assumptions these planners make about how the world will be in fifty or even twenty-five years are hard to predict, let alone plan.

This is a good argument that misses the point. If we force ourselves to think in time-frames of 100 or 200 years we are better able to think in terms of ten, fifteen, and twenty years. For most managers in the West, five years seems like a long time, ten years an incredible stretch. But to those who have participated in planning on a much longer time-frame, five and ten years seem easy. Also, the five-year plan can be made more relevant to the longer-term direction of the company once managers have participated in a thought process that expands the time-frame over many decades.

Twenty years ago, Honda, Canon, and Komatsu were tiny in comparison to the industry giants GM, Xerox, and Caterpillar. But now Honda makes as many cars as Chrysler. Canon has as much global unit market share as Xerox, and Komatsu has developed into a multi-billion-dollar company which not only cuts into Caterpillar's market share with its earth-moving equipment but has also expanded into industrial robotics and semiconductors. Global expansion has come from the ability to think big, think long term, and think smart. Were these organizations dominated by short-term management decisions, they would never have been able to achieve such an astounding success.

For many organizations in the West, long-term planning seems like a luxury. The plans they do make themselves are less about organizing the business and more about propaganda for banks, shareholders' annual reports, and public relations. Usually the plans do not take into consideration the structural conflicts that are driving the organization away from where it wants to be. Hardly anyone thinks about changing the structure because management is caught up in a reactive/responsive pattern of oscillation which is driven by a long-/short-term structural conflict.

True long-term planning that is capable of focusing the organization on well-conceived end results will be restricted as long as this type of structural conflict is in play. CEOs will come and go, but unless they can change the organization's underlying structure, none of them – no matter what their management style or temperament – will be able to create more than minor shifts of oscillation.

Structural conflicts in the new management style

We hear a lot about new management style these days. Cross-functional teams are said to break down the walls of miscommunication and encourage people to think more systemically. Decision making is being pushed down further into the organization and becomes decentralized, transforming what was autocratic management into management of a consensual type. What was once proprietary information is not distributed throughout the organization. As stock options are made available to the members of the organization they are encouraged to think of themselves as owners. Managers are also encouraged to treat their people with dignity and respect, and the employees' health and general well-being are promoted as a high value which will lead to company loyalty. All these trends sound enlightened, indeed. Yet when many organizations attempt to implement these practices the byproduct is often confusion and instability.

A common complaint of senior management is that people hesitate to make decisions once they have been given the authority to do so. Another is that although cross-functional teams have productive work sessions, their actual plans tend to be put on hold. Though members are encouraged to think from a wider organizational perspective, they still think and act out of local concerns. With all the talk about how people should be treated and act, political intrigues still dominate the scene. Why are these good ideas about management not always as useful as they should be? The answer is found in the structural conflicts that determine an organization's behavioural tendencies.

Decentralizing decisions

In the past, organizations had excessive layers of management that served to centralize control. Decisions were made by people who were not always close to the situations that those decisions affected. This unwieldy situation burdened many organizations with slow response times and unrealistic plans.

To many organizations, it began to make sense that those who are affected by decisions should be involved with the decision-making process. Their judgement should be the soundest and since they were involved in making the decision, implementation should be more effective. It was hoped that more people making decisions at strategic locales in the company would lead to more managerial capacity. So in recent years, many organizations attempted to decentralize their decision-making process.

This change was a more radical one than it first might seem. Decisions are a medium of *power*. By pushing decisions down into the organization, power is being distributed more widely. More power everywhere means less power concentrated into the hands of a few. Also, those who succeeded in their careers as managers did so because they knew how to make decisions themselves. They kept a large degree of control in their own hands, for that was the method that assured them that things were being done properly. Most managers see themselves as responsible for maintaining control of the work processes.

When decision making was decentralized, successful managers were asked to relinquish some of their control. Many of them found this hard to do. Here is the structural conflict that managers and the people they manage faced.

A manager's desire to control outcomes leads him or her to make all major decisions, which are then implemented by other people in the organization.

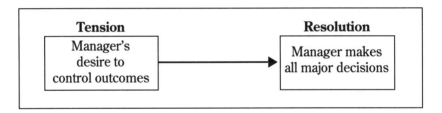

But the manager may lack vital information that people closer to the situation confront daily. This leads to a desire to have those very people able to make decisions so that they can address immediate concerns in a timely way.

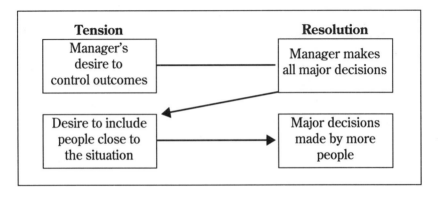

But when more of the decisions are made by more people, the manager has less control over outcomes. This situation feels unstable to many managers. Tension builds on the manager. Soon the manager's desire to control the outcome becomes dominant again, and he or she reclaims the power to make all major decisions.

More people making decisions leads to less control. Fewer people making decisions leads to more control. The result is an oscillation between centralized and decentralized decision making.

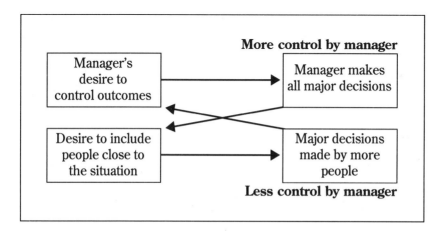

What of the people who are given the new power to decide? We would expect people to seize the opportunity of playing a bigger role in their organization. Surprisingly, they often do not. Many people are uncomfortable with their new power and avoid making decisions. Why?

When we are given decision-making power we are also given a degree of accountability. We may fail. Most organizations do not know how to deal judiciously with failure. Failure is usually an unforgivable mistake that leads to punishment of one sort or another. When that's the case, everyone avoids making mistakes.

Decentralized decision making goes hand in hand with widely distributed accountability. The potential threat of failure increases proportionally with the new-found power, and people are *less* likely than before to make decisions because of the potential danger.

Here is a structural look at the phenomenon:

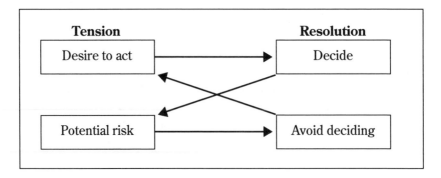

People want to act so that they can participate in the enterprise. But when they begin to make decisions the *risk* factor increases. They resolve the risk by avoiding making decisions that are potentially hazardous. From the structure we begin to understand why people seem to be behaving in inconsistent ways. The forces in play are changing and the people act accordingly. They are, in fact, responding quite naturally to a built-in conflict within the organization.

The growth–stability conflict

Decentralized decision making is designed to support growth within an organization because when there are more people who are able to decide, an organization's management capacity is increased. Instead, it often leads to oscillations between growth and instability. An elegant structural description of this behaviour is found in a structural conflict between *growth* and *stability* that can lead an organization to a pattern of behaviour which oscillates.

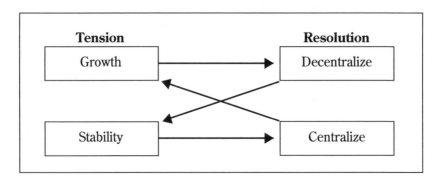

In this structural conflict the desire for growth leads to the decentralization of decision making. However, even if growth occurs, it creates instability. Once there is a shift of dominance, stability becomes more desired than growth, and decisions are centralized again. From a structural perspective, the conflict between growth and stability creates pronounced non-equilibrium, which is not discrepant with the structural motivation to restore equilibrium, resulting in limitations in both growth and stability.

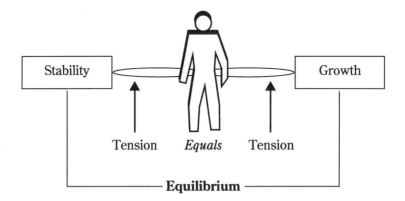

This conflict could be avoided – as we will learn in Chapter 4 – by better organizational structural design in which stability and growth goals are developed together within the context hierarchies.

Layers of structural conflicts

Usually, several structural conflicts are occurring simultaneously within a single organization. The *growth–stability* conflict often co-exists with conflicts of *change–continuity*. The *invest–cut costs* conflict may be added to the mix. *Decentralized centralized decision making*; *autocratic consensual management styles*; and *short-term–long-term conflicts* add even more layers of structural conflicts overlapping each other.

The patterns of oscillation may take several years to repeat and may move so slowly that it is difficult to pinpoint just what is causing the changes, but the inexorable pull of the structure is felt by everyone.

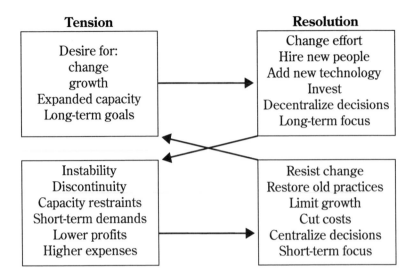

The meta-impact

When several structural conflicts are in operation simultaneously there is often an experience of desperate struggle, as people fight against movement that seems beyond their managerial control. Moreover, there is another more subtle impact that penetrates the organization – resignation and hopelessness. There is a feeling that nothing works, and that fate, more than imagination and diligence, will decide the company's future. Changes in leadership may temporarily suspend the collective experience of fatalism, but if the structure remains unchanged, the honeymoon with any new leadership is soon over, and people return to a profound sense of powerlessness. Only this time it is even worse than before, because a glimmer of hope has proved to be merely an illusion. Management may try to shake the organization out of this type of malaise. It may try to instill positive thinking, a motivational furore into the organization: 'C'mon, everyone! We can do it! We only need to believe in ourselves!' Or it may try a 'slap in the face' approach in the hope that the organization will come to its senses and say, 'Thanks. I needed that.' Temporary benefits may result from either of these methods, but neither will succeed long term. Carrots and sticks are unable to change inadequate structures and we must begin to think in terms of redesigning the company's structure so that change will lead beyond chronic patterns of oscillation.

4 Structural redesign

The air, these days, is filled with terms that imply the possibility of instituting organizational change on a *structural design* level: reengineering, organizational architecture, restructuring, and so on. The words have an important ring, so naturally many people are using them for marketing their training and consulting services. Unfortunately, however, these terms are often misleading because the concepts that they represent are not based on a real structure. They have merely been borrowed from disciplines which do deal with real structures – engineering and architecture.

When these terms are used indiscriminately to describe *non*-structural content, banal marketing rhetoric distracts us from true insights which are essential for real and lasting organizational change. We must not confuse our exploration of the topic of *structure* with tired old organizational concepts dressed up in new language or with irrelevant, pop-management hype that happens to use similar-sounding terms.

Structure deals with the *relationship* of elements to each other and to the whole and with the influence that these relationships have upon behaviour. We have seen that structural conflicts produce oscillating behaviours. How are we to deal with these behaviours and with their underlying structures? The principle is that *rather than attempt to fix inadequate structures, establish more suitable ones.*

A more suitable structure than *structural conflict* is *structural tension* which produces *resolving* behaviour. The difference between the two structures is that structural conflict is formed by the competition of *two* tension-resolution systems; structural tension is composed of only *one* tension–resolution system. To demonstrate how we can use this principle in a structural redesign, let's revisit the change–continuity structural conflict by way of example.

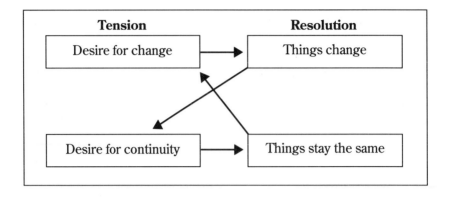

In this structural conflict change begets a desire for continuity which leads to the avoidance of change. But once continuity has been re-established, the desire for change re-emerges. In order to move from structural conflict to structural tension, we first need to identify what we really want: *what is our desired outcome? What do we really want?* In this case, we want *two* outcomes, both *change* and *continuity*. But to the degree we change the organizations, continuity is lost, and to the degree we hold on to continuity, the change effort is resisted.

Hierarchy of importance

While both of these two goals may be important to us, *one will be more important than the other.*

• *Change* may be more important than continuity.
• *Continuity* may be more important than change.

Consequently, we must create a *hierarchy of importance.* First, we need to determine our *primary goal* – the one that is more important than its competing goal. Once we have done that, we can organize a new structure and a new structural tension.

Change itself is a process that is conceived to serve some particular result or desired outcome – one that would be accomplished once the change effort has been successfully completed. Before creating a hierarchy we must be clear about the desired outcomes of the change effort. Why do we want to change? To improve our products? Our management systems? Our relationship with suppliers? To expand our market share? Develop customer loyalty? Or, better, our efficiency and effectiveness?

Once we have answered these questions we need to evaluate our current level of continuity. Organizations are in the habit of constructing strategies for change without considering the degree of continuity they want to maintain while the change effort is being implemented. How much continuity do we need to maintain? How much discontinuity can we live with? Once we answer these questions, we can form a continuity goal.

Since the desire for change leads to a departure from the norm, our continuity goal will be formed by our change goal. However, we may find that our change goal is impossible to achieve in the short run because the resulting discontinuity may work against us. This situation provides us with an opportunity to rethink our desires. Which is more important to us:

- Fast change which may be disruptive to the organization?
- Or a longer-term implementation of change that will help us to maintain a consistent level of continuity?

If we need to accomplish change in a strategic time-frame, we might choose to pursue our change goal, knowing full well that continuity will be undermined. Of course, we would not want a prolonged period of discontinuity, but we might decide to permit the situation to exist temporarily.

If our change goal does not need to be accomplished immediately we might decide to build a firm base of organizational continuity, paving the way for the transition before we attempt drastic change. In this case, our continuity goal will be senior to our change goal, and we will regulate change by continuity.

The following example serves to illustrate how and why a company might choose continuity over change. In order to increase the sales volume the sales and marketing departments of a large pharmaceuticals company formulated a plan to change their marketing approach radically. Instead of a single nation-wide strategy with each product line marketed by a different sales force, they proposed to use fewer sales people selling a greater variety of products to doctors, and to developing local marketing strategies that would be tailored to each geographical area. Their idea was based on two major considerations: that each area of the country had a unique consumer mix (Florida, for example, has a larger retired population than most other parts of the USA) and that doctors do not like to be besieged by a plethora of sales people.

The sales and marketing departments were enthusiastic about their ideas, and held a meeting with senior management to propose the plan. Senior management rejected it almost immediately, not because the idea was poorly conceived, but because they were unwilling to adopt an unknown and untested marketing strategy over one that was generating the company's major revenue source. The change might have worked brilliantly, but management did not want to put the economic continuity of the business in jeopardy.[1] Their interest in continuity was greater than their interest in change, even though the change was designed to increase the sales volume. Change in the marketing strategy would need to be organized in the context of economic continuity and utilize such things as pilot programmes in selected regions, or single experiments to study the efficacy of the strategy.

Either change or continuity can be of higher value, but they cannot be equal. Therefore, we need to determine which is the more important value. Once we do that, we have created a hierarchy. We have determined our primary goal. *Our primary goal will be the focal point in organizing structural tension, the other goal will be designed to support it.*

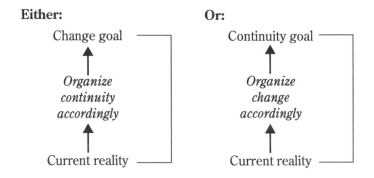

Either: **Or:**

Change goal   Continuity goal

Organize continuity accordingly   *Organize change accordingly*

Current reality   Current reality

---

1 Many organizations have damaged their economic base by managing change haphazardly. Their relationship with customers can suffer when change of products occurs or services are disrupted. The most famous example of this disruptive change is when Coca-Cola changed its formula and loyal consumers thought that they had been betrayed. But there are many other examples. When Jaguar changed the classic curvaceous lines of its XJ6 saloon car and gave it a boxy nondescript design consumers also felt betrayed.

When we move from structural conflict to structural tension, we are defining our more important objective – our primary goal. The goal in the *competing* tension-resolution system is then reorganized to be *supportive* of the primary goal, rather than conflicting. If change is our more important goal, for example, we will be prepared to manage the resulting discontinuity that may occur so that we can better support our change effort. If continuity is our more important goal, we will manage any change efforts in such a way that are not significantly disruptive. Once we know our primary desired outcomes, we can organize competing outcomes accordingly.

Remember our growth–stability structural conflict?

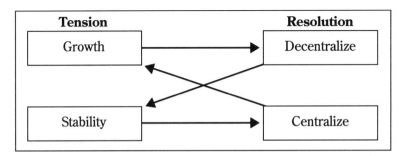

Once we determine which is more important to us, stability or growth, this structural conflict can be converted into structural tension. Then we can redesign the structure by establishing goals that reflect our hierarchy of values – and support it by managerial counterbalance.

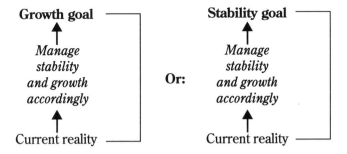

Most structural conflicts in organizations can be addressed by establishing hierarchies. But establishing hierarchies is not all there is to the process of structural redesign. We must also put into place new structures that support our aims, our aspirations, our ambitions, and our purpose.

The key to organizational redesign

The key to organizational redesign is creating a *structural tension* in which we identify the *desired state*, know the *actual state*, and organize our actions strategically so that we can move from one to the other. Because most organizations are fragmented into divisions, desired end results created on the local level often conflict with the goals of other divisions. Even cross-disciplinary management teams often fail to align various local goals within a company-wide context because of the other, more powerful, structural factors in place, driving people to set local above organizational concerns. Reward systems; power, position, and turf issues; competition for the same resource base; confusing and contradictory evaluation systems and political intrigues all take their toll. Even when people want to cooperate with each other, the structures that are in place can drive their behaviour to work against cooperation. We must first consider, therefore, the largest and most basic building blocks. We can then move from the level of the most general and broadest unifying concepts – *why are we in business?* – to the divisional, departmental, and project team level – *what do we need to do locally to help the company to fulfil its purpose?*

Step one is accomplished when the organization knows what it wants. This apparently simple recognition can be a tall order for many companies. Clarity of purpose is rare. Most companies suffer from unclarity of cross-purpose. Is its purpose to survive? To thrive? To lead the market? To pay back the stockholders? To make products? To serve customers? To expand into other businesses? To build an empire? To provide a living for its members? To invent technology? To change the world? Those in leadership positions feel the effects of contradictory concerns most deeply as they attempt to balance the various demands that vie for their attention.

The most effective leaders are able to become *senior* to the pressures that come from competing interests, not by compromising the direction of the company through trade-offs and politics *but by moulding and shaping the organization towards a well-defined future*. Part of their job is to transform structural conflicts into structural tension by determining hierarchies. Part is to stay focused on the organizational aspirations. Part is to become fluent in the current reality as it applies to their company, their industry, and their world. Part is to evaluate the effectiveness of the strategies and tactics being used.

Leaders know where they want to go. Furthermore, they *use* their aspirations as their primary organizing principle. They have – I hesitate to say the word because it has become so trite and platitudinous in recent years – *vision*. They have a clear picture in their minds of a desired state, and they govern their actions accordingly. Without a clear end in mind, direction is impossible.

The bankruptcy of the vision, purpose, mission statement

Vision must not be confused with a vision *statement*. Most organizations have a vision statement, a purpose statement, or a mission statement. But very few of them have clarity of vision, purpose, and mission. Ironically, the fashion of constructing statements can work against a true sense of vision, purpose, and mission for the statements are often compromises on the part of the people who write them. The statements themselves have usually trivialized the organization's most meaningful concepts through weak, watered-down, simplistic declarations. This is due in part to a technical flaw in the approach that organizations commonly use.

Teams of people sit in rooms at off-site locations and ponder the reasons they exist as an organization. They gain valuable insight and often begin to experience a sense of what might be described as the organization's higher calling. So far, so good. But then they are charged with the task of putting that sense of spirit into the confines of one phrase, sentence, paragraph, or statement. This task would be hard enough for the world's greatest poets, let alone those who are relatively inexperienced in translating complex ideas into words.

The resulting statement usually tells us little about the organization's vision, purpose, or mission. Instead, it is an awkward expression of vagueness:

> We are the company that has the most advanced technology in widget design, is recognized for being the industry leader in quality, has high market share with totally satisfied loyal customers, in an environment where people are able to develop their talents and abilities by meeting the challenges of today and tomorrow, while producing extremely high profitability.

Once statements like this are placed on metal plaques around the building, other members of the company begin to wonder about those in senior leadership positions. Notions of vision, purpose, mission, and values can take on the scent of snake oil awfully fast.

Which would we rather work for, a company that had a vision statement, but didn't have a vision; or a company that had a vision, but didn't have a vision statement? Of course, we would all choose the reality of a vision over the mannerism of a statement. Even an organization which has a true vision can rob that vision of its power by reducing it to a slogan. Think of how much richness and profundity is lost in slogans such as 'God is love', 'Hug your kids', 'Make love not war', 'Celebrate life', etc. While God may be love, and it is nice to hug our kids, much is missing from these slogans. Where is the mystery and power of the religious experience as reported to us by the saints and mystics? Where is the deeper love that a parent has for the child, the joys and fears of the first solo bike ride, the constant struggles for a clean room, the poignant dull pain that comes from their first school term away from home?

In our age of slick television ads we have come to believe that short, pithy statements say something worth listening to. But slogans do not tell the whole story. Many of the most important ideas with which we organize our lives are not reducible to a single statement.

Real vision is better expressed in ways other than vision statements – in consistent actions over time, in quality products, in the actual spirit within the organization, in the aspirations of the company, in the way it connects with the world, and in the accumulation of thousands of experiences that the organization generates.

When vision is talked about, it is better done through discussing and exploring ideas, and encouraging the participation of other members of the organization in the vision's realization, rather than sloganeering.

Many organizations are unclear about their own aspirations. While they hold on to silly slogans, any serious critical thinking about their deepest desires eludes them. This makes it difficult to build structural tension into the essential architecture of the company. Consequently, structural conflicts are more apt to rule their fortunes.

An organization that does understand its direction and purpose is a different matter entirely. All decisions can be measured against this standard. Are they consistent with the purpose of the organization? From disciplining the organizational intent by policy design that is consistent with organizational purpose, they can align action with aim, learning with need and aspiration, and direction with desire.

Let's take a look at what we need to know and understand in order to change from an oscillating behaviour pattern to a generative one.

A clear reason to exist – purpose, vision, mission

Why does the organization exist? There may be several reasons, but not all of them are important. We could say that it exists to provide income for the employees, or to provide products or services to customers. We could say that it is an institution which has some internal meaning in and of itself. We could say that it exists for the pleasure of the stockholders.

While there are many practical reasons why any organization exists, there are also other types of reasons – cultural, social, and spiritual: to provide a way of life, to contribute to the development of society in general. The spiritual reasons may be a bit more obtuse, but they are more profoundly causal than any other type of reason. They deal with what we might call the organization's 'higher purposes'.

While the spirit of something may be hard to describe in concrete terms, it has a tangible reality that permeates an organization. An organization's spirit influences everyone.

The spirit should not be confused with the structural nature of the organization. In the best of all worlds an organization's structure and spirit will be consistent and reinforcing, and one of the goals of our organizational redesign is to match the spirit and the structure. To do this for the organization, first we need to identify our prime reason to exist.

Our prime reason to exist

Identifying our prime reason to exist is not as difficult as it may sound. It's relatively easy once we have overcome our tendency to be shy about our true, altruistic motives. For many, especially for those in leadership positions within an organization, deeply held values are important, not simply as a moral code but as a way of life. These are people who aspire to accomplish that which matters to them. Their ambition is not merely a game in which the stakes are power and money; it is to change the world for the better, to enable people to satisfy the human instinct for building, exploring, and creating.

People in leadership positions are also practical. The message they have received early in their careers is to downplay their altruism because it seems to contradict an aura of managerial shrewdness.

During off-site meetings through the facilitation of a good consultant, a group of people can explore their personal values as well as the deeper desires they have for their organization. They can see if there is a match between the spirit of the organization and the values that matter most to them. This is best done in small teams involving both senior management and other principal members of the company. Questions like 'Why do we exist as an organization?' or 'What is the purpose of this company?' help to focus the inquiry.

At first, it may feel unnatural to speak of things that matter most. Some people in the group will be impatient and uncomfortable. The subject may seem intangible and some may feel that the group is wasting valuable time that it should be spending on more important items – the five-year plan or budgeting. Others are embarrassed to reveal just how much they care about the organization, and some are threatened by such talk and avoid questions that may lead to a deeper understanding of their own lives. These embarrassments are only temporary, however. Soon, the process of questioning centres the discussion where it belongs, on identifying why the company exists in the first place.

It is hard to organize our lives around something that doesn't matter to us. The same principle is true of our organizations. It is difficult to organize the company around things that don't matter to the people involved. Not only is it important that those in prime decision-making positions know the organization's deeper reason to exist, they must *care* about it themselves. *Once the purpose is clearly understood, it becomes the basis for forming the organizational super-structure – structural tension:*

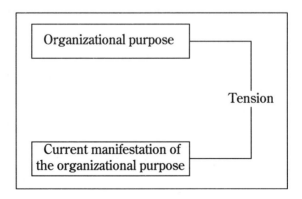

The organizational purpose is a dynamic principle in developing policy design, strategies, and the structural make-up of the company. It is *the* senior organizing principle and as such, it can be used to discipline all major decisions. Understanding the major governing idea behind the organization provides us with the ability to put all decisions to this test: Are they consistent and reinforcing with the company's purpose?

Marketing ideas within the organization

Once we identify the organization's reasons to exist, we need to position these ideas so that they will govern the large-scale strategy for the organization. How do we communicate these ideas to those who were not in the room and who will not have had the same intensity of experience that we experienced in contemplating the organization's deeper purpose? This is a marketing job, and the market is the employees of the company.

As we have said, it is important that we do not attempt to turn meaningful ideas into platitudes. It takes more than a slogan to communicate our deeper values. Furthermore, slogans work against us by presenting our values in a simplistic light that leaves them subject to ridicule and disbelief. Would we attempt to express the love we have for our children by putting up posters in their rooms? 'Remember, kid, Daddy and Mummy love you!' Or do we attempt to express our love in countless actions that support our words?

It may be best for the people involved in the meeting that explores these issues *not* to talk about the concepts they have developed. Most of us have had the experience of a management group going off to the mountain of organizational enlightenment, partaking in a peak experience, and then descending back into the organization – wide-eyed and inspired. These managers are often 'sitting ducks' for misunderstanding. Rather than spread the word, their enthusiasm discredits it. Everyone else waits it out until those under the spell cool down and come back to earth.

Their experience may be real, *but experiences do not always translate into resolve*, and once the heat of the moment is over, so is the determination. Experiences come and go, but our true values will not be subject to regressions. Here is the principle:

Motivation is sustained by deeper values rather than peak experiences.

It is easier to talk about these values once they are supported by actions, policies, strategies, and rewards:

Deeds communicate the values more effectively than words.

How can these new ideas and values best be communicated to the organization? Usually through a combination of ingredients:

- Through changes in people's actual orientation and motivation
- Through discussions that explore the ideas
- Through comprehensive and consistent policy design
- Through implementation of the policies
- Through the efficacy of the new ideas
- Through a groundswell of increased interest in the concept

Above all, the fundamental ingredient that is unparalleled in influence is to *mean* what we say and order our lives accordingly. Reality is more persuasive than all the propaganda in the world.

Meaning it, however, is only a first step. If the structure and systems within the organization work against the values of the corporation, it will be hard to act in ways that are consistent with our governing ideas. Structural conflicts may dominate the company to such a point that talk about the organization's most meaningful governing ideas leads only to increased oscillation. When this is the case the structure must be changed from structural conflict to structural tension by re-examining the organization's policies, strategies, rewards, and practices. Do they reinforce or contradict the organization's purpose and values? How do they need to be changed? Often there is an immediate cost associated with these types of changes. The proof of sincerity is demonstrated by the organization's willingness to invest in the changes needed.

The business of the organization

Once we have identified why we exist as an organization, the nature of our business must be redesigned to support the organization's purpose.

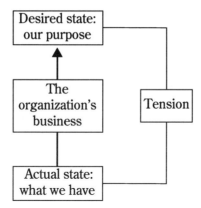

Formulating a clear business strategy

A business strategy describes how the organization generates wealth – how it makes money. A management strategy describes how work gets done through the coordination of various resources – and departments. Business and management are different disciplines which require a different set of skills and abilities. When this distinction is not made, the function of each discipline becomes obscure, and policies are often designed with built-in structural conflicts between competing forces. Ironically, many otherwise good managers are not skilled business people. They have not run businesses, designed long-term business growth strategies, or had total responsibility for the organization as a successful business. Managers in charge of the success of their area from a purely management, not business, focus can organize their efforts in favour of a local frame of reference that can hurt the company's business. Those who make decisions must have some overall knowledge of the business strategy of the organization. When they do, the decisions they make can reinforce and support the design.

How does the organization make money? A company that produces wealth by competing for market share will have a different business strategy from one that does so by developing a small niche in a larger market. A company may generate wealth by bringing new products to market, and therefore investment in product development may be essential in the business design. The company may generate wealth by its investment strategies, and therefore economic tactics will be closely designed and managed. Quality of service may be an essential factor in a market that is quality sensitive.

The business strategy will lead to policy designs used to organize decisions into a comprehensive and consistent reinforcing framework. Since decisions will define the hierarchy of importance among competing elements, they had better be based on sound business sense.

Many organizations adopt a 'shotgun' approach to their business strategy. 'Let's do it all!' 'If one thing is good, then more are better!' Product development, niche markets, financial investment, total quality. The built-in deficiency of shotgun strategies is that they weaken organizational critical thinking. If *everything* is good then individual elements of a strategy become arbitrary. The relationship of various factors is dulled, and everything is made to compete for the same resource base. Resources become squandered. Actions cancel out other actions.

A good test

The test of a good strategy is: Do the steps taken make it easier to take the next steps? ... and the steps after that? A good strategy has direction – it moves from one place to another. A good strategy generates more and more energy; it creates momentum. A good strategy relates the parts to the whole; every action works with all the other actions. This is why a targeted strategy is superior to the shotgun approach. It focuses the organization, generates an economy of means, and leads to important hierarchical decisions.

To help managers develop their strategic business skills we divide the participants of some of our courses into two groups. Then we give each group a business scenario. For example, both groups may be in the semiconductor business, but one group will be in the commodities end while the other group will be in the 'designer-boutique' microchip end. This is the only information the two groups are given, and then they have twenty minutes to develop a business strategy. Frequently, the people in each group spend their time in *managerial* rather than *business* discussions. Often goals are created that show no understanding or relationship to how the company makes money. Typically, people will say things like 'We will increase sales 25 per cent next year'. 'We will dominate our market internationally'. 'We will increase our profit margin to a 23 per cent return on investment'. The extraordinary thing about these discussions is that these types of goals were created in a vacuum. Increase compared to what? Return of investment in relationship to what? When participants were asked what they were attempting to accomplish with these types of goals they weren't able to answer. They didn't know. Why would they come up with these kind of goals? Because they have developed the habit of evoking business rhetoric whenever they are asked to create targets.

To many of these people *business strategy* does not refer to how the business *generates* wealth. Some of these managers were in the habit of forming business goals that were merely an extrapolation of the previous year's performance. 'If we sold 20 000 units last year, let's sell 20 per cent more this year.' This is not a real business strategy because it doesn't tell us the *mechanism* by which the increase will take place. But it often passes for one.

The practice of developing some business goals then creating tactics that are intended to achieve those goals is one of the bad habits many managers have developed. This is why they often fail to understand how their own organizations work as *businesses*, let alone how to construct a business strategy within our semiconductor scenario.

After their first experience with the semiconductor exercise we give the participants another chance to develop a business strategy. When the managers were able to rethink the semiconductor scenario they considered *why* a customer would want to buy the product. Within the commodities end of the business customers buy from their suppliers for two reasons: the products are *fast* and *cheap*. Quality is not a factor as long as the quality is truly adequate. Customers want the price to be low so that they can lower the price of their own products, making them more competitive. Customers want fast delivery so that they can meet their production schedules. *Fast* and *cheap* leads to a network of other decisions: where manufacturing plants should be built, how transport and delivery systems should be organized, how costs and pricing should be determined – the beginnings of a solid business strategy.

The strategy for the designer-boutique microchip end of the industry was quite different. *Why* do customers buy these chips? Innovation, design, and quality of engineering. Since these chips are custom tailored to be used in specialized products, price sensitivity is less important than design quality and innovation. This business strategy must be designed with engineering, innovation, and uniqueness of function in mind. Our company would invest in developing its capacity for invention. It should offer high salaries and create working conditions that would attract the very best and most creative engineers. It should invest in extensive research and development programmes. It should market itself by promoting an image of engineering brilliance and the reliability of its design innovations.

This exercise has helped many managers to rethink the basic business assumptions of their own organizations. They begin to see the tapestry of decisions that are logical outgrowths of the business strategy. They now have a criterion for creating hierarchies, and therefore they can now form structural tension out of structural conflicts.

Unless a company understands the fundamentals of its business strategy it will be unable to design consistent and productive management strategies. A good test in evaluating the level of comprehension of the business strategy in an organization is simply to ask several members of the company what the business strategy is. Watch out for platitudes, stock phrases, and banal generalities such as 'customer focused and highest quality'. They say nothing about how the company generates money. In fact, often these types of expressions mask a shallow understanding of how the company works as a business.

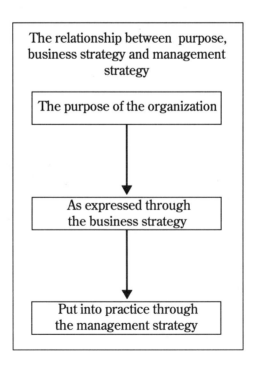

Each element can be designed into a structural tension form and arranged hierarchically. The management strategy serves the business strategy, which in turn serves the purpose of the organization.

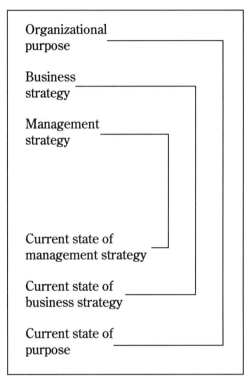

The organization's offerings

How does the organization create and disseminate its offerings – its products and services? The system of dissemination will be the vehicle for transmitting its deeper values to the world. The following questions can help to establish clarity:

- What is our offering?
- Who are our customers?
- What do they want?
- What do we want?
- What is the match between what we and the customers want?
- How do they know about us?
- How do they obtain our offering?
- What is the current market?

- What is the future market?
- How will our offerings change?
- Where are we going?

These straightforward questions help us to focus on:

- What we should do
- How we should do it
- How it will work – viability
- Where we are going

Too often, questions like these are answered in such a way that they fail to lead to a comprehensive understanding of overall strategy. If you were to ask several different people in the same organization the questions listed above they would usually answer with regard to their local area but would not be as fluent in the workings of the overall organization. Without the broader context of a comprehensive, organizational design, conflicts of local interests will plague the company.

Everyone who makes decisions within an organization benefits from understanding the overall design of the enterprise. This *meta-dimension* helps to organize decisions into consistent frames. The local levels of the organization can be arranged to support the more senior levels in the structural hierarchy.

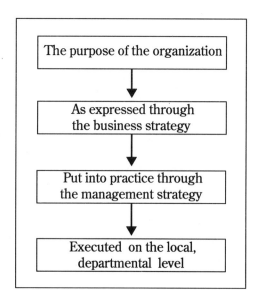

The organizing feature of structural tension is then used to tie departments to the other dimensions of the structure:

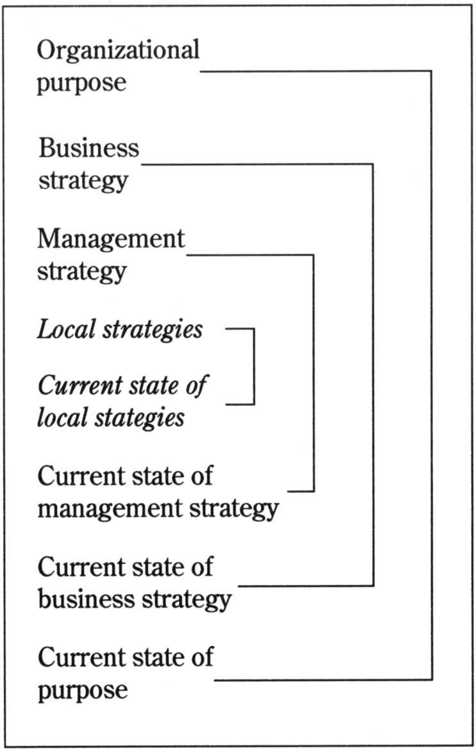

Organizational
purpose

Business
strategy

Management
strategy

Local strategies

*Current state of
local stategies*

Current state of
management strategy

Current state of
business strategy

Current state of
purpose

Progression

Once structural tension is established, actions can be organized to
bring the desired outcomes into being. The actions can be developmental so that we can increase our energy and momentum. Learning
and creating are tied within structural tension, and the result is an
economy of means. We learn how to create what we want through
the most efficient and effective process – *one that is self-correcting*.
Not only are we able to improve the process by which we accomplish
our desired outcomes, we do so *as* we take action. The learning is
progressive and leads to improved understanding, practicality, and
mastery.

Structural tension is the essential frame for action. However, structural tension does not exist in a steady state. It is a *dynamic* state in which shifts of degrees of tension increase or decrease based on the degree of discrepancy within the structure. The greater the difference between our vision and our current reality, as there is in the beginning of the creative process, the more the tension. The closer current reality moves toward the vision, as is the case in later stages of the process, the less the tension. However, as the tension moves toward resolution, momentum increases and it becomes easier to continue in the direction we have been moving. We add to the momentum through increased quality and effectiveness of action over time.

Within structural tension, we build a *progression – movement* from something to something. The progression has the following characteristics:

• Consistency of motivation
• Repetition factor
• Continually increasing capability
• Continually increasing capacity
• Continually increasing effectiveness

Within the frame of structural tension, actions are taken.

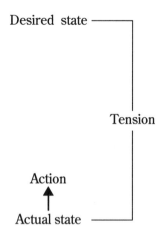

The action produces a consequence or an immediate result:

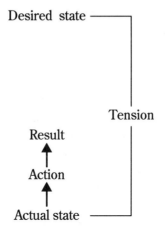

The result is evaluated from a structural tension perspective. Did the action help the actual state to move closer to the desired one?

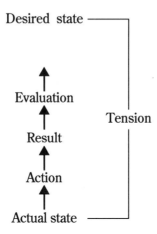

From our evaluation, we adjust our future actions:

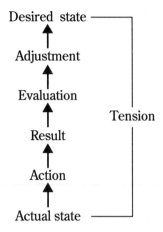

The cycle repeats itself until the desired outcome is achieved. As the cycle repeats, a change occurs. With each repetition, more is learned. Greater understanding and experience lead to greater effectiveness. We are able to take better actions, producing better results, conduct better evaluations, which lead to better adjustments, and so on. The progression is refining and strengthening the process.

Action–result–evaluation–adjustment–action–result–evaluation–

Beginning capability   **More capable**

Adjustment–action–result–evaluation– adjustment–action–result –

More capable   More capable

Evaluation–adjustment–action–result–evaluation– adjustment–

More capable

The right structure for the job

Within the frame of structural tension, progressions of action–results–evaluation–adjustments lead to increased capability. But not all improvement leads to a progression. Take the incremental improvement some have used in their attempt at instituting total quality approaches. We begin with the current condition, analyse it, and then improve it.

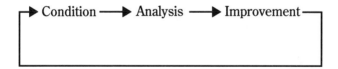

Where is the driving or generative force within this process? It is found within the current conditions. What is the analysis designed to do? Find imperfections within the current conditions. What is the improvement designed to do? Eliminate imperfections. Over time, fewer and fewer imperfections will be found as the improvements work. Instead of building momentum, the process is moving towards inertia as the driving force or generative energy reduces.

One of the best aspects of many total quality approaches is that an entire system of relationships is considered, rather than simply local events. However, many people involved with TQM lose their system-wide focus over time. As people begin to work with incremental process improvements, ironically, the overview is often lost.

Another structural conflict that is often found in organizations attempting to use a *condition–analysis–adjustment* cycle is as follows:

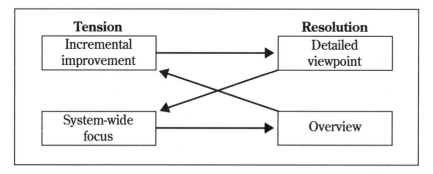

In this structural conflict, the oscillations travel between a narrow focus on process to a broader focus of the larger system. People feel torn between both polls. The structure is inadequate to produce what we want – incremental improvement *within* the context of the whole.

Another interesting structural conflict demonstrates why many incremental improvement approaches have actually inadvertently stifled invention and creativity:

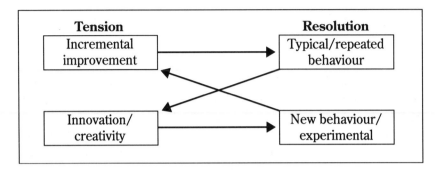

As Andrea Gabor writes about this condition in her book on Dr Deming, *The Man Who Discovered Quality*:

> The formalism of policy deployment and TQC can, in some extreme instances, foil innovation. By the late 1980s, a mangement heretic at Toyota, which has won more quality prizes than any other company in Japan, would say that conventional TQC is too inflexible to be applied effectively to the creative, often spontaneous business aspects of marketing, such as developing advertising campaigns and wooing clients...
>
> Fuji Xerox managers also complained of the limitations of TQC. Some Fuji Xerox managers were hinting that the rigid way in which TQC requires that every management move be justified with data may have inhibited laboratory creativity and impeded basic research.

Oscillations between typical and experimental types of behaviour arise out of the competing tension-resolution systems in the above structural conflict. As we move towards typical behaviour of variance-free processes we begin to feel as if we are in a rut, and innovation is sorely needed. The theme of the organization shifts from TQM to innovations. But as innovations are tried, new variations and unpredictable behaviour emerges that fall outside of our desire for minimal variance.

Of course, we want useful inventions *and* we want reliable processes that support those inventions. What is interesting is that in many organizations these two desires are positioned against each other, and the result is limitation to both process improvement and invention.

Redesigning the structure

From the structural perspective if we found that a structure was inadequate for our purposes we would attempt to design a new structure that enables us to achieve what we want. In the condition–analysis–adjustment cycle we can redesign the structure *by creating a higher-order form of structural tension.*

First we need to locate our desired end result. What do we want? This question needs to be considered from a broader perspective than simply 'the best quality possible' or 'customer satisfaction'. In fact, when incremental improvement is adopted within an entire TQ approach that is tied to rigorous systemic improvement, higher-order goals – such as minimal production variation tied to customer loyalty – *can* be the starting point of a more rigorous exploration of desired outcomes. This change is not merely tinkering with problem-solving techniques. Rather than the goal of eliminating defects, the improvement process will be motivated by concrete desired outcomes.

So-called *zero defects*, motivated by problems within current production approaches, do not lead to new processes that are more efficient, cost effective, or innovative because they do not help us to define the desired end results. Motivations based on knowing what we want functions quite differently from those based on eliminating what we do not want.

One of the obvious weaknesses of most management systems is that goals are developed in isolation from overall strategy. The question 'what do you want?' is often answered from a local viewpoint that is so narrow that the goals may be arbitrary or contradictory within the broader context of the organization. In what ways does our interest serve what we want for our organization, our business, our market, our customers, or our industry? What is our *greater* vision for our enterprise? What do we want our future to be? How do we tie the local goals into the management strategy, into the business strategy, into our purpose? Any process that we choose should align the focus and deepen the magnitude of our organizational concerted effort.

Once we know the answer to these questions we can begin to build structural tension by defining our vision and our current reality in relationship to that vision:

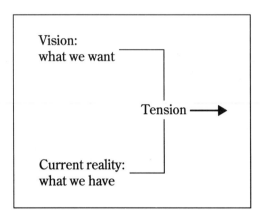

Within that structural frame our quality-improvement process will transform from producing inertia to producing momentum, because the higher-order structure is giving rise to the tendency to resolution.

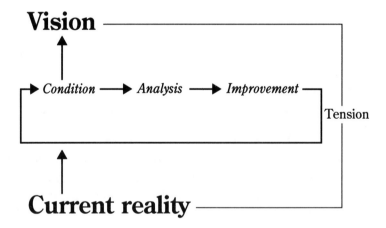

We have changed the structure, and now the process for improving quality *builds momentum*, rather than forms inertia, through the principle of progression.

Many organizations adopt various processes that are not tied to desired outcomes. Although these practices are thought to improve the workings of the organization, since the result they are designed to serve is unclear, a *refinement* of the process is impossible, as is significant learning. If we don't know the results we want, we will not be able to create clear standards of measurement to use in evaluating current reality. When measurements are unclear, how do we know how and when to act? We don't. And so we must wait for a crisis to show us what actions to take. However, these actions cannot help us to arrive at a desired destination. At best, we will have eliminated an undesired situation.

Those organizations that succeed brilliantly at a total quality approach are framed within structural tension, and systematic improvements do not happen in a vacuum. The desired outcomes are clear to everyone who is working on the improvement of processes. Current reality is studied well by accurate statistical measurements and other types of instruments of observation and analysis. Process improvement serves an identifiable result which helps to define relevant standards of measurement.

Unfortunately, many organizations who have attempted to adopt a quality approach, re-engineering, or other fundamental change strategies fail to understand that they may need to reorder the underlying structural realities of the company. Without structural reinforcement, the organization's underlying structure works against the best attempts at improvement and change. At the end of the exercise, most people within the organization are frustrated and discouraged while oscillating behaviour is shifting at its highest degree of magnitude.

Without a frame of structural tension, many adopt a process system that does not seem to live up to its promise. Was the process flawed? Often not, at least not in principle. It is simply misunderstood. The disciplined thought process that needs to go into such an undertaking has been ignored and unexplored. When that happens, all we can do is take on process steps in the most superficial manner, which would discredit even the most formidable approaches for accomplishment.

The two questions that must be addressed thoroughly are: 'What do we want?' and 'What do we have?' *Every action must be tied to these questions either directly or indirectly. If actions are not tied to the answers to these questions, what, then, is their purpose?*

Leadership

Leadership has many forms and personalities, but one common function of leadership is that leaders help us to know where we want to go and where we are currently. In other words, structural tension is the basis for greater leadership. Every great leader has had the following in common:

- They knew where they wanted to go – the desired end result.
- They knew where they currently were.
- They cared deeply about the end result.
- They were able to encourage others to join with them in the creation of the result.
- They were able to help others to focus on reality in relation to the desired end result.
- They were able to translate structural tension into actions that were designed to move from current reality to the desired outcome.

When we think about great leaders, we often think of the likes of Winston Churchill, Gandhi, Martin Luther King, Jr, John F. Kennedy and other charismatic personalities who seemed able to capture the imagination of millions of people. In our television age leadership can seem tied to an appetite for celebrity status. But this impression is inaccurate, particularly in organizational leadership. Organizational leadership does not require the magnetism of an extraordinary television personality, nor the mystique of a historic figure. Some of the most effective organizational leaders might not stand out in a crowd, or thrill the multitudes merely by their presence, but nonetheless they are able to inspire in others a profound desire to build a desired future by joining together.

More than in government and politics, the playing field for leadership is the organization where management and leadership fuse into action, movement, and accomplishment. Management and leadership are not always identical, but both are important. Some leaders are not good managers, and their leadership suffers from their lack of managerial understanding. Some managers fail to lead the people they manage, and so they are limited in their ability to propel their teams or divisions towards greater achievement. Within our organizations, we need managerial leadership.

The best form of managerial leadership combines leadership deftness with management technique through a frame of structural tension. Once structural tension has been established, the managerial leader orchestrates action plans that are designed to bring clear end results into being.

Principles can help to define desired end results

- *Start at the end.* What is the *outcome* we hope our actions produce? How would we recognize the result we want? What does it look like? What is it? How does this result support the management or business strategy? We can better understand what we want once these questions are answered.
- *Quantify whenever possible.* It is better to assign numbers to the description of the result whenever possible because it gives us more clarity about the desired outcome. If we said we want growth, what kind? How much? Let's use an example that we might find in a sales and marketing department within an organization. For the sake of our example, let's assume that the organization has clearly defined its most important governing ideas, its business and management strategies, and has targeted its long- and short-term plans. As part of this, the marketing people want growth of sales. When they are asked to define their desired end result, they might state the obvious:

  First draft: We want more sales. This does not give us a very clear picture of the desired outcome. 'More' is a *comparative* term. When we use comparative terms we are not able to locate an end destination until we do some more figuring. *More* will always be *more, less, less.* The phrase 'more sales' begs for *more* information. What are the current sales? How many more do we want? etc.

  Perhaps we say we want a 20 per cent increase in sales. This is closer to a real number, but it still does not tell us how many sales we want within what period. We need to calculate the total and define the time-frame. If sales were a million units per year, then we can more easily describe the end result we want.

  Second draft: 1 200 000 units sold this year. The second draft is much clearer. This goal may now be the basis for structural tension.

End result

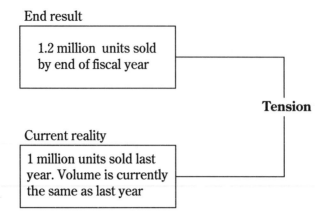

Tension

Current reality

- *Use dates when possible.* Not only is it a good idea to use numbers, it is also advantageous to use dates. By *when* is our result desired. This helps to frame the result within the context of a specific time period. It gives the numbers additional clarity.

The action plan

Once we establish structural tension we are ready to design an action plan. By describing our desired end result and current reality well, the action plan becomes easier to form. In the following example the order of consideration was as follows:

1   The desired end result
2   The current reality
3   The process – how we move from here to there.

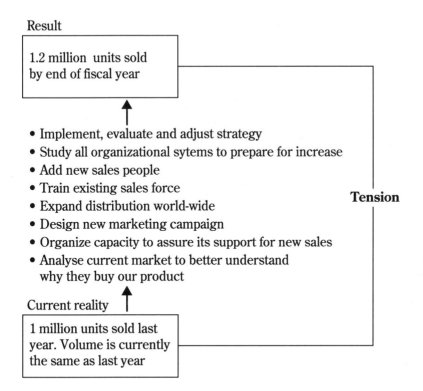

Result

1.2 million units sold
by end of fiscal year

- Implement, evaluate and adjust strategy
- Study all organizational sytems to prepare for increase
- Add new sales people
- Train existing sales force
- Expand distribution world-wide
- Design new marketing campaign
- Organize capacity to assure its support for new sales
- Analyse current market to better understand
  why they buy our product

Current reality

1 million units sold last
year. Volume is currently
the same as last year

Tension

The outcome tells us *what* we want, current reality tells us *what* we have, and the action steps tell us *how* we plan to move from here to there. The actions describe general activities that contribute to the desired outcome of 1 200 000 units sold. Each action point can be evaluated, adjusted, and managed. We can place many actions into a time-frame, and that makes them easier to organize strategically.

```
┌──────────────────────────┐
│ 1.2 million units sold   │
│ by end of fiscal year    │
└──────────────────────────┘
```

- Implement, evaluate and adjust strategy – *ongoing*
- Study all organizational sytems to prepare for increase
  – by 1 February
- Add new sales people – *by 1 March*
- Train existing sales force – *by 1 March*
- Expand distribution world-wide – *ongoing*   **Tension**
- Design new marketing campaign – *design by mid-February*
  implementation begins 1 March
- Organize capacity to ensure its support for new sales
  – by mid-January
- Analyse current market to better understand
  why they buy our product – *due 1 February*

```
┌──────────────────────────┐
│ 1 million units sold last │
│ year. Volume is currently │
│ the same as last year     │
└──────────────────────────┘
```

These action steps are described in very broad terms. However, each step can be telescoped into another frame for structural tension. For example:

- Design and implement a new marketing campaign – designed *by mid-February. Implementation begins first week of March*

can translate into:

- Desired outcome: New marketing campaign design – *by mid-February*

If we were managing the sales goal (1 200 000 units sold annually) one of the *actions* we would take would be to commission the new marketing campaign. If we were in charge of marketing, the new campaign might be one of our *end results*. Some action steps (how we get there) become new end results (where we want to go).

```
┌─────────────────────────────────────────────┐
│ Desired outcome:                              │─┐
│ New marketing campaign – designed by mid-February │ │
└─────────────────────────────────────────────┘ │
                                                 │
                                          **Tension**
                                                 │
┌─────────────────────────────────────────────┐ │
│ Current reality:                              │ │
│ Marketing campaigns in the past have been     │ │
│ moderately successful. The current campaign   │ │
│ has had the most impact on sales. The combination │─┘
│ of print ads to television has produced 23% more │
│ new inquiries turned into sales. The budget of ads │
│ is limited, as are in-house human resources (and so on) │
└─────────────────────────────────────────────┘
```

Notice that current reality includes information that is both positive and negative. In our description of reality we can include our advantages and our disadvantages, as well as other types of relevant data.

Once we have established our new structural tension we can fill in the action plan:

> **Desired outcome:**
> New marketing campaign – designed by mid-February

▲ • Write a second draft for ads – *by 8 February*

  • Test copy and ads with various focus groups – *by 5 February*

  •Schedule ad space in appropriate media – *by 1 February*

  • Write copy for ads – *by 1 February*

  • Hire a designer for print ads – *by 1 January*   **Tension**

  • Get current ad rates – *by 7 January*

  •Do a statistical analysis of current campaign – *by 15 December*

> **Current reality:**
> Marketing campaigns in the past have been
> moderately successful. The current campaign
> has had the most impact on sales. The combination
> of print ads to television has produced 23% more
> new inquiries turned into sales. The budget of ads
> is limited, as are in-house human resources (and so on)

In turn, some people in our department may translate some of our action steps into their own structural tension forms as they move to accomplish their mandate.

Every action within our system has a defined result it serves. Every adjustment is relevant to structural tension. Every end result may be understood from the frame of other end results which may be senior to or subsets of the one we are considering. Everything is related, strategic, and integrated.

Of course, this is a simple example. We really see the power of structural tension as an organizing force in difficult management situations. A typical example is as follows. One of my clients, a pharmaceutical clinical research group, was in charge of an anti-AIDS drug. We held several days of planning sessions, and determined the overriding end result of the project, which was FDA approval if the drug qualified. This end product was charted in a structural tension form as the current reality was studied and reported. Out of that, there were twenty-six major strategic action steps that were needed to accomplish this goal. The twenty-six steps were then organized into their own structural tension charts, with each step telescoped into a new end result with its own set of action steps. In turn, each of these steps was also telescoped out into end results, which were then made into another set of structural tension charts. All told, there were over 150 structural tension charts for the project. The manager of the project worked with two of her people to coordinate all the various activities. One manager's job was to govern each of the structural tension charts in a kind of project manager's role. He would keep the projects on track in terms of timing and allocation of resources. The other manager's job was to coordinate the fit of all the activities, making sure that the parts would integrate with each other. They created what they called 'the war room' where every structural tension chart was hung and used as the basis for coordinating the project. Structural tension charting became a practical method for managing an extremely complicated project, which factored in the various uncontrollable elements such as test results, new scientific discoveries, and safety issues.

A strategy for renewal – reliable systems that continually revitalize the organization

Organizations never reach a Newtonian, homeostatic steady state of consistency. They are dynamic and changing. How will change come about? Will it be planned or unplanned? Will it be haphazard or composed? Will it be positive or negative?

Too much of the time, motivation for change within organizations comes from problems, difficulties, or conflicts. When born of such impetus, change will be temporary in its effect. Once the conflicts are reduced, the motivation will fade. Since people do not plan to have problems, these changes are also unplanned and introduced haphazardly into the organization.

The topic of fundamental change may give us the impression that once this basic change is accomplished, the organization will reach an ideal state, and the change effort will no longer require consideration. But in reality, the work is not over once the fundamental change is achieved. The campaign simply transforms into another sphere of progression.

Change can affect an organization positively or negatively. Our chances of a positive effect are better if we are in control of the change effort. The way to do this is through a strategy of disciplined movement towards the organization's goals.

Incremental change is helpful in quality development. But by itself it will not serve continually to revitalize an organization. We must do more than improve and perfect. We must be on the move. We must be going where we want to go. We must create, build, grow, transform, streamline, and aspire.

We need to stay in touch with the generative force that endows the organization with its vital essence. After they mature, organizations often become stodgy and complacent; they merely attempt to maintain what they have. The greatest companies stay current and are always looking to the next horizon. In so doing they are in touch with the most generative characteristics of the human spirit – invention, exploration, creation, higher purpose.

Organizations are able to evolve into greatness if they bear in mind basic principles of *continuity and stability, aspiration, higher purpose, consistent systems of management, current and future relevance.* Organizations often fail when they lose their interest in aspiration and higher purpose.

Design for greatness

What is the relationship between leadership and organizational greatness? True organizational greatness is not over once an outstanding leader has left. As in great civilizations, the power to expand and build is deeply integrated within the organization. Great organizations can outlive their leaders, while lesser organizations cannot. Why?

- Power is distributed widely and well.
- Consistent relationships between local interests and overall interests are soundly managed.
- The organization itself is a social force.
- Principles determine policies.
- Expansion is clearly defined.
- Resources are managed in ways that are consistent with the comprehensive design.

How can real strategic planning be accomplished if a company's broader purpose for the process is unclear? How can people sign on for the long haul when inducements for collective actions are vague? When we recognize the deeper aspirations we have for our organizations, this vital force motivates all our actions – from the most mundane to the most important. Renewal is best accomplished through consistent and reliable systems that continually refocus the organization on its generative spirit.

Methods that produced success need to be continually rethought

Some practices that were used to create past success may continue to be valid, some may not. How do we know the difference? We must stay in touch with our general organizing strategies and study their efficacy.

Many organizations make the mistake of assuming that methods that worked in the past will work in the future and will continually work well and do not need to be re-evaluated. As an organization expands, the best comprehensive design can slowly and invisibly deteriorate. Too often, we lose touch with the game plan as more immediate issues dominate our focus. By continually rethinking our overall strategies we will not tend to fall into that trap. Rethinking our methods is not limited to senior management. Everyone can participate in continually assessing organizational effectiveness.

A clear method for course correction

It is not enough to change when a situation demands it; that will always be too late. Change must be anticipated. One method of anticipation is to construct contingency plans. However, most contingency plans are ineffective because they are problem based.

It is better to form contingencies based on desired outcomes. Once desired outcomes are defined clearly, a variety of possible changes in reality can then be considered. Most of the imagined conditions will not happen. But having thought them through, we are much better prepared for the terrain of the future.

Current effectiveness

We can also correct our course by examining our current effectiveness. When systems do not work well we are apt to define the situation as a problem, and then use methods to solve the difficulties. This is a limited type of course correction. But it has little lasting value to the organization. Often, it is a sign that inadequate study has gone into implementation methods and execution.

Ongoing consideration of how well we are implementing our strategies needs to be arranged as a feedback and learning system. One of the most chronic failures of most organizations is lack of useful information. While we live in the *over*-information age, much of the information we receive is irrelevant. Too often, people in organizations fill out forms, collect data, and file information that has little meaning and consequently the information goes unused. Perhaps much of it is not useful. We can better separate the relevant from the irrelevant if we have clear standards of measurement.

The following are some questions that can help to bring this issue into focus:

- What do we need to know?
- When do we need to know it?
- What does the information mean in relationship to our organizational goals?
- What adjustments are needed?
- What are the goals of the adjustments?
- How will we know if the adjustments worked?
- Who needs to be involved and when?
- What general principles can we learn that will be useful in the future?

Consistent course correction requires a formal system of review, not a search and destroy mission. If course correction is an ongoing process many modifications will take place *before* the situation degenerates into a problem. Small adjustments, after all, are much better than large ones.

A clear system that continually aligns people

People can fall into and out of alignment. We often assume that once we achieve a degree of accord with people within our organizations it will continue intact. But it doesn't always. Shifts in demands can alter a person's focus. When alignment is assumed but unaddressed we can lose touch with it.

Therefore it is wise to create a system that continually aligns people with their true caring about the governing ideas of the organization. Such a system will keep the focus on our values, purpose, and so on.

In Asia many organizations begin the day with rituals designed to establish and reinforce the governing ideas of the company. In the West we have morning meetings, newsletters, video presentations, and so on, but we tend to think informally about alignment. The results are often hit and miss. What is necessary to create alignment?

- People who share the same values
- People wanting to work together towards common outcomes
- People who are members of the organization by their own conscious choice.
- People who are motivated by a deep desire to contribute to the organization
- A fair game (one in which people can succeed or fail based on the merits of their actions rather than political intrigue)

When these factors are present, alignment is more possible, but even then, it is not guaranteed. We need to rekindle alignment often, by establishing formal methods dedicated to that purpose.

A clear reward system that reinforces organizational values

One of the most disruptive forces in an organization is a reward system that is inconsistent and contradictory. Rewards, more than words, define an organization's values. Rewards tell the members of the organization what is desired of them. They come in many forms from economic to symbolic and imply various theories of motivation – ideas about why people do what they do.

Created by various people who may have cross-purposes and mixed methods, reward systems are often haphazardly developed. Rewards are designed to encourage or discourage certain types of behaviour, but the conceptual frame is often limited to local concerns rather than overall organizational design. We will explore this important issue in greater depth in Chapter 5.

A clear learning and training method

Training is a powerful instrument for change and for strengthening and extending capacity. However, most companies do not appreciate the opportunity that training presents. Partly this is due to the lack of a clear direction with regard to training. Training programmes, like reward systems, tend to be put together haphazardly and represent mixed points of view and unclear mandates.

Both in-house training departments and senior management are to blame for this condition. If we had to put the mistake they make in one word, it would be *piecemeal.* Too often, training does not have a comprehensive purpose that is integrated into the comprehensive, organizational design. Consequently, people get training that may be irrelevant to the greater organizational cause. At other times, the information they receive contradicts previous training they have been given within the same curriculum.

Usually management training is seen as separate from the overall business strategy. But for a training method to be successful it must reinforce both the management and business strategies through consistent continuity of subject area and relevant skills.

In work with many training departments, our company has helped them to redesign their training approach such that it reflects and reinforces the overall goals of the organization. The basic principles we addressed are:

- Defining the general business strategy
- Defining how the managerial strategy supports it
- Defining what the training goals are
- Dividing training into basic and specialized programmes
- Evaluating the current offering
- Eliminating training that is inconsistent with the overall strategy
- Adding training that reinforces the overall strategy
- Designing an overall curriculum
- Marketing the new comprehensive training strategy in-house
- Staying in close touch with various managerial levels to monitor the success of the approach

Many people think of training as classroom learning. But it can and should be much more than that. For training to be directly useful, it must translate into actual work-related actions. If a manager takes a course and walks away with useful concepts that do not result in a direct application, from the organizational point of view the training method has failed.

The best possible training is on-the-job. When limited to course work, training can seem abstract and theoretical. Yet many training departments offer an assortment of courses that are barely translatable into work-related applications. At the end of the exercise, people feel that training, while perhaps interesting, is not a terribly good investment of their time.

In one of our client's companies, the training department revamped their entire approach and developed a comprehensive curriculum that led to three types of in-house MBA programmes. Their training method went from a confused mix of contradictory course offerings to a streamlined and effective learning strategy that reinforces the business and organizational strategies.

The approach we used was to study the expressed values of the organization, particularly the general business strategy. We then developed a list of characteristics which included business and organizational design. We then divided the list into six general categories and gave them names that attempted to capture the spirit of each focus:

- *Innovation* – R&D, new products, etc.
- *Current window of opportunity* – developing the organization's capacity in relationship to its long-range strategy
- *Dynamic organizational resource management* – how to create an economy of means, cost-effective strategies
- *Collaborative spirit* – team and group building and creating
- *Professionalism* – self-generation/self-learning, skills
- *Departmental/system* – local/organization integration and development

We then evaluated every existing training programme in terms of its support of the overall business and organizational strategy and developed criteria for accurate evaluations and quick adjustments. Then we evolved training goals in each area *and tied them into the general business strategy*. We then met with many of the key players who would be the end users in this integrated approach, and received valuable feedback and insights. They also offered to help to pilot the programme.

Training became useful to the organization in ways it never had before. The process represented a major shift in the company's approach, from a catalogue-based style of unrelated course offerings to a comprehensive training strategy that was related to vital business and organizational issues. This redesign was cost effective, too. The training department was able to produce a much better training programme for about $200 000 less than its original budget.

Most people think about expanding capacity as a matter of adding more people or buildings, computer systems or machinery. But one aspect of adding capacity that is not often considered is that of helping people to improve their ability to work together. Many managers think that managerial skills are simply a matter of common sense or intuition. Perhaps, having attended many less than useful management training courses, they cannot conceive of training as helpful to their situation. However, *the right type of training* can be as important a factor in adding capacity to the organization as might be capital investments in new factories or technology. One of the most important competitive advantages that exists is the ability of the organization to learn, grow, and develop. When training is used fully and effectively this powerful resource can help an organization to reach new heights of achievement previously unimagined in the most cost-effective way.

Theme and variations

In music, film, novels, painting, dance, and architecture most works are organized around a theme – that is, a central unifying idea. Themes are used to tie together the various aspects of the work. Without a theme, it would be hard to unify the events that take place in the piece.

An organization can be unified by a theme and variations on a central theme. Within complexity, unity can be created. All decisions, policies, strategies, tactics, and the actual day-in–day-out work that people do can and should have a direction towards a central unifying purpose – the organization's theme. As in music, an organization will have counter-themes that contrast and thereby support the theme. Variations on the theme can work to add dimension and depth. In an organization that has consistent thematic unity all actions have a purpose within the greater context of the company.

When we think of organizational redesign we must think in thematic terms – our purpose, business strategy, and so on. How do they fit? What is each element's role and function? How do they affect each other? In an organization which is well designed we could go to anyone and ask them 'What are you doing?' and they would be able to tell you. 'And why are you doing it?' and they would be able to tell you from the point of view of the organizational theme. That is the mark of an organization that is well designed – the people know what they are doing and how it fits into the bigger picture.

5 Motivation

Why do people do what they do? What is their motivation? The way that an organization answers these questions leads to specific organizational policies and practices that have an enormous effect on how that organization operates. It can also lead to structural conflicts within the organization and to useless patterns.

Let us start with some very basic observations about motivation:

- People do what they do for a variety of reasons.
- There are many theories about what motivates people.
- There is no general agreement among 'experts'.
- People may have many explanations for why they do what they do, but these may not in fact describe their true motivation.
- Without understanding what really motivates people, rewards that are designed to motivate them may fail to reinforce intrinsic, self-generating incentive, and even work against it.
- Leadership can influence motivation within an organization through its governing ideas, reward systems, hiring practices, training methods, and policies.
- The underlying structure of an organization will influence motivation.
- Changes in the underlying structure will lead to changes in organizational motivation.

Survival

Many people are motivated by threat. Only when their survival seems in question do they organize themselves to take action. The threat can be immediate and physical as on a battlefield or it can be subtle, existential, and imagined. In either case, threat means danger – there is a possibility that harm will result.

We take action in order to avoid the harm. These actions are designed as strategic manipulations that will give us some degree of control over a possibly devastating situation.

If our survival seems in question we will be very careful about our behaviour. We may survey the situation in order to know what is expected of us, then respond accordingly. This is the same strategy many 'good' students have learned: 'What does the teacher want us to say? OK, then I'll say it.' In this case, the threat is not physical survival, but the intensity can seem as great. Notice that, within this strategy, the level of participation will be limited, as will involvement.

A motive based on threat and survival, like one based on eliminating problems, produces an oscillating behavioural pattern. More conflict leads to more action designed to reduce the conflict. Once the conflict is reduced, less action is produced.

Managers who attempt to manipulate their people by threats always find that, while they can generate a quick response, they cannot move towards long-term goals. Also, their efforts to control through conflict are eventually neutralized as the threats themselves become normal and predictable. People get used to them, and the threats no longer motivate them to act with the same degree of concern. When that is the case, it takes more and more hysteria to mobilize people, certainly not the kind of manipulation that will support an organization in the long run.

Situational motivation

'We will create an environment in which people can . . .' We have all heard phrases like that, uttered by people who believe that *situations* are causal forces. In many organizations it is assumed that people are motivated by situations and can be managed accordingly.

When people are motivated by the situation they have two choices. They can react or they can respond to the circumstances in which they find themselves. Therefore the circumstances, not their desires, are the dominant factor driving the action.

If an organization attempts to motivate people by changes in the situation it must have complete control over that situation. But situations can change by themselves, and often quite quickly. Many of the major variables that are in play are not within a manager's control. These include: values, character, aspirations, not to mention individual compensating strategies towards inadequacies, and so on. Because of these factors, situational motivation cannot be relied on long term.

Self-esteem

With the advent of pop-psychology the self-esteem craze has hit the ground running within many organizations. The idea is simple enough: people do what they do in order to feel good about themselves. When self-esteem is fostered within our organizations we attempt to deliver a message of elevated worth and exalted self-esteem to those whose lives are supposed to centre around the need for personal reinforcement of their precarious identities.

What is wrong with this picture? Some obvious and some subtle implications.

According to this theory we are hungry to pander to our feelings. We are supposed to experience such glorious reinforcement by managerial praise that we will increase our performance at the drop of a 'well done'. but shifts in our emotional life occur at regular intervals. Sometimes we feel better than at other times. If our involvement is determined by our emotional state, what do we do on bad days? Can a manager be expected to provide authority in the inner lives of those who are managed? Of course not.

If we do what we do for the purpose of bolstering our egos it would be difficult for us to be *involved* with the actual work in which we are engaged. *We devalue the thing itself that is being done*. The message that is inadvertently given is that the creation itself doesn't really matter, so long as it provides strokes to the ego. Yet how can we involve ourselves in something that doesn't matter? We can't. If we were to translate this message more accurately around the organization the walls would be filled with slogans that read 'What you are doing within this organization is only incidental to what really matters, how you feel about yourself'.

Managers often find that their attempts to implement the self-esteem notion work against professionalism and learning because standards become personal and subjective, rather than organizational and objective. If our goal were merely an emotional return on investment it would be difficult to address our mistakes and inadequacies – information that may have to be addressed in order to get the job done and provide the individual and organization with essential learning.

Satisfaction

A close cousin to motivating through self-esteem is motivating through satisfaction. Here it is assumed that people do what they do in order to get a sense of satisfaction and fulfilment. Personal satisfaction as a motive again implies that the actual end results of our actions do not have intrinsic merit.

Of course, we all enjoy a sense of satisfaction when we can have it. But are the great organizational achievements really accomplished by clusters of individuals seeking personal gratification? If so, how do we perform on days when we are not satisfied?

Many organizations have adopted the idea that their job is to provide satisfaction to their members. This puts the organization at a disadvantage. People are sometimes satisfied, but more often they are not. Satisfaction, while pleasant, is not necessarily a virtue, nor dissatisfaction a vice. It is good to remember that many of the most accomplished people in the history of civilization were not always satisfied individuals.

Using either self-esteem or personal satisfaction as motivations limits involvement to those projects that are likely to bring an emotional return on investment. Why?

- It is hard to predict what projects will bring personal rewards.
- Therefore motivation is tied to speculation.
- But perceptions change.
- And, as a result, the motivation to stay with a particular project drifts into inconsistencies.
- Also, managers who attempt to motivate by emotional rewards unwittingly conspire to devalue the *intrinsic* worth of the subject matter of the involvement.
- Unclear standards by which performance is measured lead to subjective evaluations of reality – how it feels, rather than how it is.
- This makes learning, evaluating, adjusting, and improving difficult.

Control

Many managers seem to be motivated by an almost obsessive desire for control. This type of obsession is definitely out of vogue these days, and so the desire for control is sublimated into more suitable behaviour, behaviour that seems more socially open and genteel. In many cases, the obsession has simply gone underground.

Why do people want control? Are they, at heart, power-hungry dictators that secretly want to rule the world? Are they psychologically depraved, needing to complete their relationships with their fathers or mothers? Are they overly ambitious and calculatingly insensitive? Probably not.

Since the focus within many organizations is on behaviour, rather than the *causes* of behaviour, a person with a control strategy is criticized without being understood. The person attempts to change – to be more open to others, to be more inclusive, to trust people, to let go of many tightly held controls – but over time, the person reverts back to his or her controlling state.

Why do managers gravitate towards controlling behaviour? Because of certain unexplored assumptions that they hold true. Indeed if these assumptions *were* true, it would make sense to adopt a strategy of control. The assumptions are as follows:

- Negative consequences may occur if there is a potential for danger.
- People cannot be trusted – perhaps their integrity can be, but certainly not their judgement.

- If people were left to their own devices they would create great harm.
- Therefore people must be protected from harm they may not even know exists.
- The manager (or whoever else holds these assumptions) must take charge for the greater good of everyone.

Those who have a control strategy do not think of themselves as others may see them – as manipulative and power-wielding. These people see themselves as good people who are simply misunderstood. They do not want power or control. They just want to protect everyone, and they feel that letting go of their power will lead to harm. Since they are motivated by a fear of negative consequences, telling them to change their ways does little to change their strategies.

For us to understand such people we must not presume that they are in love with power. Often they do not want to be controlling at all. In order for us to gain insight into the causes of the behaviour strategy we should explore reality together; we should address their assumptions.

Fear of negative consequences

Every situation has a potential for danger whether we act or not, but what is the *reality* of the danger? To a person who has a control strategy, the danger is *conceptualized*. In other words, the *actual* danger is ignored and *imagined* danger is substituted. Then any danger, real or imagined, becomes magnified. The imagination simply takes over and produces more and more conflict about what could go wrong.

Any of us who are parents have experienced this. We imagine our children falling off a roof, getting into an accident, burning up the house, drowning in the pool, and so on. While dangers do exist, our *fear* of them is not usually steeped in reality but, rather, in our *concept* of reality. Controlling parents love their children and only want to protect them from harm. But often they have lost touch with reality.

What *is* reality? How much actual danger *is* there? People who have control strategies are not used to studying reality well. In most cases, their sense of danger comes not *from looking at reality* but from *not looking*. By staying in touch with reality more of the time, the tendency to control can quickly evaporate. This is as true for the manager as it is for the parent.

You can't trust people

Again, the *concept* dominates the perception. What people can't we trust? When? How? Why not? In reality, some people can be relied upon more than others. But the controlling person doesn't know who can be trusted and who can't. When the stakes seem so high, the person reasons, why take a chance?

Here, again, reality is the only place to go. What is the truth about specific individuals? After exploring reality, the control person can often judge people individually, rather than tarring everyone with the same brush.

The issue of trust is best explored after the true *reality* of danger has been addressed. If the control person imagines a looming threat, no one, no matter how reliable they may have been in the past, would pass the test of one who could be counted on. Therefore it is useful to see reality for what it is before we encourage blind faith in people in general.

Taking charge will be in everyone's best interest

'People do not know what is in their best interest,' the controlling person thinks. This type of person is often quite protective of the rest of us. Our safety is seen as more important than our freedom. When we study reality rigorously we learn that there are certain things that are beyond our control. Many things in life are simply out of the realm of human choice.

Controlling people do not know this. Instead, as they get older, they attempt to control more and more of their world. But reality, being what it is, often defeats their best efforts. They experience a sense of powerlessness which leads, in turn, to an increased sense of threat and a greater fear of the future. This gives them even more reason to want to control anything that they can. This futile cycle leads to less ability to act effectively, to create desired outcomes, and to help the organization to build increased capacity. Over time, the controlling person's strategy defeats growth, learning, and even his or her stability.

The organizational control strategy

Organizations have control strategies for the same reasons individuals have them, fear of negative consequences. Change can seem threatening. In order to control the unpredictable, policies are put forward to anticipate what might happen and how the organization should respond. Control is often expressed in an array of policies, rules, and regulations that are designed to be used in the face of any new situation.

Another, more subtle, control strategy involves class distinctions. In some organizations roles are defined and spelled out in detail so that people will know their place. There are penalties for not obeying the rules. Ethics are clearly defined, because it is presumed that people do not have proper values and would only do the 'right thing' if forced into it by an ethical code determined by the organization.

Symbolic motivation

Some people think that people are motivated by symbols. They are thought to be driven into action by attempting to win awards or hold positions that represent symbols of station in life. Reality, to these people, is less important than what it might symbolize. More and more these days, organizations attempt to motivate people by symbols, and so award-winning and fancy titles have become common themes.

For the entire cold war the United States had a symbolic enemy – the 'evil empire' or international Communism. The real potential enemy, the Soviet Union, which had directed enormous resources to the defeat of the democratic world, was only incidental in the minds of those who thought in terms of symbols. The reality was less interesting and less important to many of the cold war politicians than the symbols they attempted to use to mobilize the West.

Today, much of the criticism of Japan is on the symbolic level. To those who think in terms of symbols rather than reality, Japan is no longer a country that has succeeded in many of the areas of industry in which the West would like to succeed, but is a symbolic enemy dedicated to robbing the West of its industrial strength and resolve through cynical manipulations of Japan's enormous economic might. Many Westerners are happy when Japan has economic reversals.

Symbols are not reality, nor are they the playing field of real accomplishment. They are simply *pictures* that have been given *synthetic* meaning. But symbols can lead us away from reality, and therefore render us impotent and ineffective. Once that happens, the most we can hope for is the downfall of the competition, rather than our own growth and well-being.

There once was a man who ran out of cheese to put into his mouse trap. So he put in a picture of a piece of cheese. When he checked the trap in the morning he found that he had caught a picture of a mouse. Symbols are not the same as reality for mice or organizations.

Personal versus organizational

Within most organizations reward systems are constructed to reinforce individual performance. How are we to know if the performance is worth rewarding? How can we reward individuals when some of the best work is done by groups without individual fanfare? Indeed the best groups are so unified in their performance that the individual contributions are integrated into a seamless whole. It is what in the arts is called *ensemble*.

Here is the structural conflict between the need for personal credit and the requirements for organizational team performance:

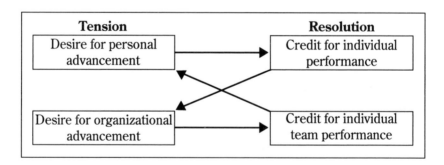

Obviously, there are competing tendencies here. The desire for personal advancement leads to a desire to stand out as an individual. How can we shine? But this is in conflict with the need of the team to flourish as a group.

Our cultural traditions and educational system reinforce the idea of individual success: personal victory, triumph, and conquest. But often the needed skills that are required to advance an organization's achievements are *group* skills.

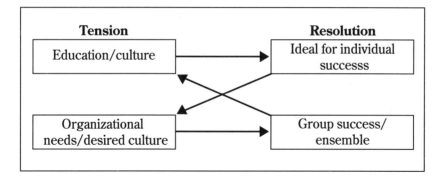

The conflict of interest between group and individual success is usually built into the organizational structure. But with a structural redesign, both elements can *reinforce* rather than *compete* with each other.

As we have seen in Chapter 4, conflicts such as these can be resolved by establishing hierarchies of importance and values. When we determine which element is of primary importance and which is secondary we are able to establish structural tension as the dominant force. Which is more important – the group or the individual?

To help us think about this we can make a 'forced choice' to better define our values. If we had to choose between personal kudos (but our accomplishment would not help the group) or group accomplishment (but we would not get any personal accolades) which would it be? Of course, we do not usually face this kind of extreme choice; however, this is a useful thought experiment. Once we know where we stand, we will be able to establish hierarchies, and they will be based on our most important values.

For the sake of the creation

The most powerful motivator for both the individual and the organization – and one that is often overlooked as concepts of pop-psychology become more and more ingrained in organizational thinking – is a desire to create a result so that it can exist. As Robert Frost said, 'All the great things are done for their own sake'.

This is not how we have been taught to think. We have been schooled in the self-serving value of some sort of 'return on investment'. When we do something we want to know what the payback will be.

Consider the following two diagrams:

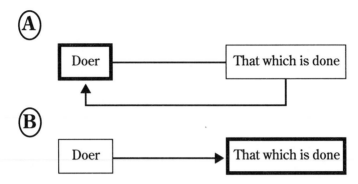

In the first (A), the focus is on the doer. What is the *point* of the participation? To provide the person who does the deed with some form of return on investment. The return might be anything – material or emotional rewards – but the payback functions in exactly the same way. The objective of the action is to provide the doer with rewards.

In our society the most common idea about motivation is that we do what we do for some kind of return on investment. Television and magazine ads show us how wonderful we will look and feel if we use their company's products. Images of success, satisfaction, riches, admiration, and love are some of the prizes that many of these ads promise. The message is simple: life is dedicated to your enjoyment. Even when people help others because they simply want to help, they can fall into the socially acceptable trap of explaining themselves by what they personally glean from helping:

'Thanks for helping us during the tornado clean-up.'
'That's okay. It was a lot of fun.'

No one likes to be a fool. We have been taught to think in terms of 'what's in it for me?' Smart people are supposed to be cleverly motivated by how well their actions balance costs-benefit ratios.

There doesn't seem to be a socially acceptable way of describing altruistic motivations. When we do try, we can seem to look like empty-headed idealists. To avoid this image we may list the personal benefits we receive in everything we do. We are trying to communicate the message that we are not fools or dreamers but rather down-to-earth individuals who know enough to look out for *Number One*. We would rather be seen as opportunistic than utopian.

Involvement

Now, there is nothing wrong with looking out for Number One. Nor is there anything wrong with being concerned with a return on investment. If we were investing money in a new enterprise, probably ROI would be the driving force behind our activity. However, the scope of our participation would be limited to how well we thought the project would pay us back. Since we would not know for sure if the investment would succeed until the final returns were in, we would have to speculate about its prospects. We would attempt to predict how well it might reward us – would it be enough to warrant the activity? Whatever our opinion was in one moment in time, our perception might change, and then our level of involvement would change accordingly. The more it looked likely that it would give us a high return, the greater our interest. The less likely it seemed, the less our interest.

In the second diagram (B) the point of our participation is on that which is being done. Not only do we care about the subject of our actions, it is, in fact, *what motivates us*. Those of us who have children know this type of motivation well. We take them to dance classes or football practice, not so they will become rich and famous and make us the pride of the town but because we love them. We take care of them when they are sick not because we hope that they, in turn, will take care of us when we are old and grey but because we love them. We involve ourselves in their lives not to manipulate them into symbols of our good parenting but because we love them. Our focus is on *them*, not us. The point of our actions is to support them in their lives in ways that are independent of rewards.

Is this principle translatable to the corporate world? Yes. Of course, the emotional affiliation is quite different, but taking action intended that a result be accomplished can be similar. The essence of the consummate professionalism is that he or she is motivated by a commitment to a desired outcome. 'I play the game for the sake of the game,' Sherlock Holmes said.

Often a substantial change appears to our clients when their orientation shifts from a ROI mode to one that is focused on results. They are able to be clear, objective, focused, and collaborative with each other in ways that seemed impossible previously. People who had entrenched themselves in various positions, and clashed with each other as to who was right, are suddenly able to review current reality objectively. They become interested in each other's opinions not as an attempt to manipulate the opposition into agreement but to understand why others see the situation differently. The actions they take lead to learning, which leads to increased competence and professionalism.

Within an organization people can be motivated by the prospect of a return on investment or because they care about the result itself. The test is: what is the primary driving force? There is often a return on investment when we 'play the game for the sake of the game'. We might become rich, influential, or even famous. But if these types of rewards occurred, while they may be welcomed with open arms, *they would not be the point of the involvement.* They would only be an agreeable and appreciated side effect. Creating a desired end result would still be the primary driving force.

This type of motivation may sound idealistic, but it is not. For many people, particularly the very accomplished ones, it is the reason they do what they do. All great things are done for their own sake.

When we are motivated by our interest in the result itself we are able to produce a much greater level of involvement because we are not measuring our input with what it might bring us in return. As we said earlier, while there may be great returns from our activities that is simply not the point. We are motivated by our interest in giving birth to the desired end results, and so we are able to be fully involved.

This type of motivation yields higher levels of participation, not only individually but also within teams, groups, and entire organizations. Our interest in the result gives us a kind of freedom. We do not need to protect our image, our self-interest, our position, or anything else. We can play 'flat out' as is the phrase. Why? Because the focus is not on us but on that which is being done. The motivational value is based on the merits of the result of our actions, rather than what it can do for us. The strength of the result has such merit that we are glad to participate – because it matters to us on its own terms and by its own standards.

Vision

Many 'motivational experts' point to the Apollo space programme as a prime example of a mission motivated by an important vision. From this example they claim that all we need is a vision, and we, like those who created the Apollo programme, would be driven to higher and higher levels of performance. What they miss is that: *it mattered to the men and women who were in the programme that we reach the moon.* Material or emotional return on investment did not motivate them. Because they authentically *cared* about the goals of the Apollo programme they were able to learn what they needed to learn, even when it was inconvenient, disappointing, frustrating, and sometimes heartbreaking.

For many, vision is just one more technique in a bagful of managerial tricks. They attempt to use vision as a concept rather than a reality. They see vision as merely an organizing mechanism that they attempt to use to foster group focus. When placed in this context the notion of vision is trivialized, and the word *vision* itself becomes banal. Vision is then adopted as a fuzzy and vague abstraction with little real substance. We may have witnessed the inspirational talk about the magical wonders of vision, and how it will lead us to the promised land of peak performance. But too often the thrill is gone before we even leave the lecture hall. Why? Because little can come from *abstract* notions about vision.

Real vision

A vision is more than merely a picture of how we want the future to be, for that is just a daydream. A real vision has at least two components: an image of a future wanted outcome and the desire to bring it about. Real vision is concrete, tangible, clear and it is tied to action. We not only want it, we want it enough to work for it. Therefore it is *the* authentic driving force that continually motivates us as individuals and organizations into exceptional achievement.

An organization that is driven by a clear vision of what it wants to create is significantly different from one that lacks a vision of its future. Without clear vision we may become confused. Why are we doing what we are doing? Do we care about what we are creating? Are we motivated by our dedication in *its* birth?

When people have conversations about vision they may think they are speaking about the same concept because they are using the same word. However, they may be worlds apart. For those who think of vision in the more amorphous, vague, and abstract sense, vision is hard to understand let alone use as a motivational force. How can we take action in favour of something that we can't quite pinpoint? We can't. So the concept of vision degenerates into some lofty-sounding emptiness which is more capable of creating cynics than high performance.

Shared vision

Many people talk about shared vision these days, but the subject is often filled with confusion that comes from a conflict of interests between *a focus on the doer* and *a focus on that which is being done*. If we were unable to make this important distinction, we would not be able to separate the notion of *vision* from the notion of *shared*.

Often, people who talk about shared vision have their focus on themselves rather than on the vision. To them, *shared* vision takes on a distorted meaning. For example, they may assume that for a vision to be 'shared' they must have some say in its formation. They must have a degree of authorship. The implication is that the vision would not be shared if they did not originate at least part of it. But why not? One wonders what the ulterior motive would be if it mattered who created the vision in the first place.

In the arts there is a long tradition of shared vision, found in large projects such as film making and orchestral music. The professionals join together to bring a vision into being. Does the first violinist complain 'Hey, I don't know if I want to play this piece by Beethoven unless I can add a few notes!' Or does the actor say to the director 'Look, I think this Shakespeare fellow is a little dated in his language. Let me modernize the lingo, so I can really get my teeth into it.' Are these performers less able to share in the vision because they did not take a hand in originating it? Of course not. So why must it be any different for organizations?

When we truly care about the vision it matters little who originated it. If the vision mattered more to us because we had a hand in creating it, then the vision's intrinsic value must be in question, or we have our focus in the wrong place.

When people are motivated by their common intent to bring a desired outcome into being the focus on return on investment, be it material or emotional, is secondary to the more dominant focus on the outcome itself. Great advancement can be achieved and heightened team performance can be developed. Furthermore, organizational learning accelerates and translates into performance.

A mishmash of motivations

Within an organization different people have various concepts of what motivates people. Their different concepts become translated into confusing and inconsistent policy designs, reward systems, and managerial reinforcements. Perhaps the human resource department thinks that people are motivated by praise. They then tend to hire people who seem interested in praise. Once hired, a person might find that he or she works for a boss who thinks people are motivated by threat, conflict, and pressure. The mismatch creates a wider and wider gap between manager and team member. Or perhaps a person who is motivated by symbols works for a person who thinks people are motivated by money. The boss gives the employee a rise, and expects that the money is all that is needed to motivate the person. But to that person, money alone may be a poor symbol. Conflicts develop because motivational concepts are not matched to reality, nor to the real desires of the organization as expressed in its purpose, strategies, goals, and systems.

In some organizations people are forced to seek managerial titles because that is the only available means for promotion. Some people, who do not want to be managers, become 'managers' anyway. In a few organizations individual contributors who do not manage anyone may be given a managerial *title* so that they can qualify for promotion and increased benefits. This type of system values managers, not individual contributors.

When they do manage a project team or a department, often scientific or engineering managers are poor leaders because they are so hungry to participate in the actual science or technology that is being developed that sometimes they interface with the project team members in ways that create dissension and confusion. Many a project manager's hope is that the departmental manager will stop interfering with his or her work, but many individual members hope that project managers will manage rather than try to do the work themselves.

Rewards/controls

Ideas about motivation may turn into a hodge-podge of mixed messages. Beliefs that people do what they do for their egos, professional pride, symbols of worth, money, position and power, job satisfaction, involvement, and the desired outcome co-exist in a kind of unappetizing stew. They are thrown into the pot then stirred, resulting in a dish of contradictory policies that tend to neutralize cohesiveness and group effort. Yet many organizations continue to construct a shotgun approach towards motivation that misses hitting the side of the higher-performance barn.

The following charts the type of compensation that various people may use if they thought that employees were motivated by particular needs or desires. Notice how wide the differences are. Imagine what might happen when there are mismatches:

If an organization thought that people were motivated by desire/need for:	They would create rewards/controls in the area of:
Money	Compensation
Power	Position/rules/policies
Professional interest	Freedom of choice
Identity	Personal service
Fear of negative consequences	Control/conflict
Ideals	Concepts
Symbols	Awards
Satisfaction	Interesting work
Security	Continuity
Challenge	Change
Interaction with others	Work teams
Individual contribution	Independence
Career advancement	Opportunity

Motivation for the high-performance organization

The organizations that consistently produce high performance are those with a consistent motivation. The motivations of individuals are aligned with each other and with that of the company as a whole.

Not all motivations work equally well to produce high performance. In wartime the people of a nation mobilize to defeat a common enemy. Great feats of patriotism and self-sacrifice become the norm. But once the threat is over, people go back to business as usual. The performance levels achieved in wartime are only temporary. When the war is over, the motivation to work together is reduced.

The motivation that works best individually and collectively is *a focus on the desired outcome* rather than on various forms of return on investment. In the highest-performance groups within the worlds of sport, the arts, science, technology, and business the focus is always directly on the results that the group desires.

But now, the most important question concerning any discussion about motivation is *can an organization influence motivation in its individual members?*

The answer can point to one of the most telling insights about a company's future. We cannot simply say yes or no. If the organization itself is unclear about its motivation, values, and goals it is impossible for it to have the authority to lead and motivate others. If the organization is clear about these things, can it influence others? *Yes!* but it is a big job.

How can the organization influence motivation?

- By being clear about its own motivation
- By a continuous educational process that reinforces its motivation
- By constructing rewards that consistently reinforce its motivation
- By consciously orchestrating its hiring practices
- By the values it demonstrates through its actions
- By dedicating resources towards creating an organization-wide alignment
- By 'walking the talk' and 'talking the truth' about where the organization stands

With so much 'expert' input in the motivational arena over the past several decades it would seem that the subject has been thoroughly explored. In fact, motivation remains an unexplored territory for most organizations.

Until we are able to make the distinction between the *doer* and *that which is done* the topic will always seem overly complex and mysterious. Once we make that distinction, however, we can understand this simple insight: when people truly care about outcomes they can reach greater heights of accomplishment than previously thought possible.

6 The learning organization

It was my friend and colleague, Peter Senge, who popularized the notion of *the learning organization* in his book, *The Fifth Discipline*. Since its publication the learning organization has become a household word and is a very attractive proposition, indeed. It conjures up images of groups of people engaged in a collective increase of organizational intelligence, understanding, and capacity. But what is a learning organization? Is there really such a thing?

Aristotle was of the opinion that any universal type class, characterized by a common noun, is a subjective notion and not a tangible reality. To him, universal notions such as *humanity* do not truly exist except in our thoughts. He considered group classifications as a handy mental abstraction but hardly an external reality. For him, the reality was found in individual human beings. Each person is the actuality, and the group identity is merely a convenient conceptual construct devoid of fact.

To Aristotle, the organization would not really exist, except in our imagined abstraction. If he is right, there could not be a *learning organization*, for what would be doing the learning? Aristotle would answer the *individual* and *only the individual*.

Is there a reality to the popular notion of the learning organization, or is the concept a mental invention that does not exist in fact?

Plato, on the other hand, thought that universal categories have a greater objective reality than the individual. He argued that the universal is more lasting, important, and substantial than the individual. He wrote 'Men come and go – but mankind goes on forever.'

Two interesting viewpoints. We can agree with both of them when we consider the organization. Without the individual there is no organization. The organization cannot be separated from individuals but individuals can be separate from the organization. Therefore the individual has a reality independent of the organization, while the organization can only exist by the participation of actual people. By itself, it would not have an objective reality by Aristotelian standards.

On the other hand, it seems that organizations have lives of their own. They are almost like organic entities that are governed by their own principles of movement, growth, possibility, and tendency. People come and go, but the organization can exist with a different cast of characters, and even outlive them all.

So what is the *objective reality* of the organization? Within the organization, individual entities connect and lead to a greater system of relationships. This is analogous to a person when the cells of the body join together and the body itself joins with non-physical elements – such as personality, emotion, mind, and spirit – to form a human being.

Whether there is an organization in the objective Aristotelian sense of reality, the combination of the various organizational elements do seem to *function* as a single entity and act in accord with its own rules. This organizational entity has a type of personality and a type of orientation towards the world. It has its own set of values that are expressed through consistent actions over time. It has underlying structures that lead to tendencies for behaviour – both functional and dysfunctional. The entity does change over long periods of time, change often similar to the evolutionary cycle of youthful vigour into sluggish old age.

Yet the organization can renew itself and become young again, regaining its vitality and drive. It can become rejuvenated – but only if it can learn. Organizations that can't learn, can't change. Organizations that can learn, can transform themselves into new entities capable of greater heights of achievement.

The old school

For most of the post-war period, most of the learning within an organization was done by senior management. It was the senior management who grappled with the deeper organizational issues, delved into the purpose and essence of the enterprise, balanced the competing forces, broke new ground of management technique, and did most of the thinking for the corporation. 'The people on top do the thinking, the rest of the people do the acting,' the expression goes. Senior management functioned as a think tank, and the rest of the organization worked on application.

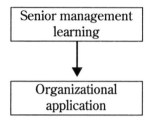

This division of labour worked fairly well when the people on top were actually learning. But, as is human nature, many senior executives gradually stopped learning; they began to see themselves as so knowledgeable about their own businesses that no one could teach them anything. During the late 1960s and 1970s Detroit car makers were convinced that they knew their business better than anyone else.

Even when senior management in an organization continued to learn, the learning did not always penetrate the rest of the organization. Individual learning is a good first step. But often individual learning does not yield an increase in the collective learning of the organization.

A change in one cell of the human body may be an isolated event that has no effect on the fundamental structure of the body. Similarly, the enlightenment of one individual or group of individuals may not lead to fundamental organizational change.

The learning organization

A learning organization is not merely a loose federation of individuals who have a high regard for learning and who happen to be part of the same organization. Rather, the learning organization is an entity that has the capacity, instinct, and inclination to learn, an organization wherein learning is everyone's affair, an organization that is alive with the possibility that something new can be born, given life, and can grow to maturity. The learning is self-generating, and not a product of desperate survival needs that have to force people into it.

Film production companies are often learning organizations, particularly the ones that stay together production after production. Steven Spielberg's company is an example. Many of the principal technical people have been with Spielberg for years. Over that time, people have increased their ability to work and learn together – learn from each other, learn as a group.

What motivates the learning? In the case of a film company it is the individual film that is being created. Learning does not happen in a vacuum, especially within organizations. When learning is tied to a desired end result it becomes an essential part of the process that produces that result.

There is a natural relationship between learning and creating. As we will see later in this chapter, if the creative process is anything, it is a learning process: learning how to bring into existence a desired end result that did not exist before you took action to create it. Organizations that are built around the creative process have a natural tendency to be learning organizations. This is why some of the best examples of learning organizations are in the performing arts, in production companies like Steven Spielberg's.

Why people learn

There are many reasons why people learn. Some reasons are more conducive to organizational learning than others. Some are more apt to be self-generating and some are not. Learning has a personal dimension that must be considered when forming a learning organization.

Learning for the sake of learning

Jacob Bronowski, the author of *The Ascent of Man*, said that *if a child is anything he or she is a learning machine*. By the age of three, children are learning and perfecting their language skills, their motor responses, their understanding of time and space. They have a natural instinct to learn. Is this a temporary phenomenon or is it an essential part of the human condition?

People love to learn, and much learning is not directed towards the accomplishment of anything in particular. Many people, for example, cherish collecting trivial information. Their joy in knowing how many dresses Madonna wears during a rock concert is self-motivated, and has no practical purpose, except perhaps to annihilate one's opponent in a game of Trivial Pursuit.

There is something inexplicably enriching about learning facts, theories, computer systems, details of historical events, and so on. This kind of learning is done for pleasure. The point of the learning is one's own amusement; it does not have to lead to anything more productive or useful.

Learning for the sake of learning sometimes results in something new – an invention, a concept, a product, a method – but if this happens it is serendipitous. Learning for the sake of learning could not, by its nature, be the basis of a reliable process. Therefore this is not the type of learning that would lead to a learning organization. Nonetheless, learning of this sort has its own pleasures and individual rewards.

Learning in order to solve problems

Much learning, especially organizationally, is designed to solve problems. An unwanted situation stimulates actions which, in turn, are designed to eliminate the problem. Learning simply functions as one of many methods intended to overcome obstructions. Learning based on problem solving is a defensive type of learning. It is learning *how to stop what you don't want*. The incentive to learn is tied to the intensity of the problem: the more intense the problem, the more incentive there is to learn. The less intense the problem, the less incentive to learn. Once the condition that stimulates the learning is over, the motivation to learn decreases.

1. High intensity of the problem

Problem

2. Leads to action taken to solve it

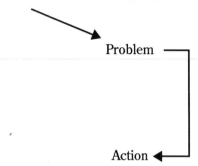

3. Leads to *less* intensity of the problem

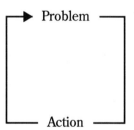

4. Leads to *less* action

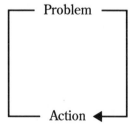

5. Leads to the problem re-intensifying if unsolved

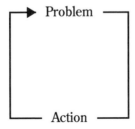

This structure leads to a predictable pattern of oscillation. More intensity leads to more action, which reduces some of the intensity of the problem, which leads to less action, which may lead to intensification of the problem all over again. In organizations that centre their management style on problem solving,[1] different problems shift in dominance over time. With each new squeaky wheel, other squeaky wheels lose their interest and importance. If action has been taken to rid the company of the problem, the intensity of the problem may be significantly reduced – even if the problem itself remains the same or gets worse as other problems take supremacy in interest and influence.

A problem-solving organization cannot be a learning organization

If problem solving is the major organizing principle within a company it cannot be a learning organization for the following reasons:

1 Learning will not be self-generating. Instead, it will be generated by the problems.
2 What is learned is limited to how to *eliminate* unwanted situations, not how to bring about desired situations.
3 Motivation for learning shifts from one problem to another as problems change in importance over time.

---

1 *Problem solving* is used in the most commonly applied connotation within organizations. Another use of the term is found in mathematics and engineering in which *problem solving* is not motivated by eliminating an undesirable condition but by bringing forth desired information, such as the sum of a column of numbers.

4 If the learning is successful, the problem will go away, leaving little application for learning in the future.
5 Often the wrong things are learned. For example, how to stop something from happening, rather than how to have something happen.
6 A false impression about learning is created within the organization – for example, that the time to learn is when there is a crisis.

There is much confusion about the link between learning and problem solving, especially since problem solving is such a common management technique. But clearly, *chronic* problem solving within an organization demonstrates a *lack* of essential learning.

Some managers become so enamoured with problem solving that they consider that their purpose in life is to find and solve problems. During the heyday of problem-based management styles in the 1970s and early 1980s many companies discovered that some of the best firefighters within their organizations also turned out to be the pyromaniacs. The more rewards that were given for dealing with crises, the greater the number of calamities that occurred. Some companies found that when they got rid of the firefighters, many of the fires went out.

Of course, organizations do have problems and do need to deal with them well. But the better designed the business is, the less likely that problem solving is its primary orientation.

In one high-tech company we worked with, the engineers assigned to customer service loved solving technical problems so much that they saw every situation as a new personal challenge, even if that particular technical problem had already been solved a dozen times by other engineers. Naturally, the company began to get complaints from their customers. Finally, senior management intervened and made sure all such technical information was systematized. Learning that had been made on a personal level now became learning for the tech service division as a whole. Common sense, of course. But it was not at all obvious to the engineers who, ironically enough, had previously thought they *were* in a learning organization because of all the learning that was going on.

The personal technical challenge enjoyed by the engineers was in conflict with the goals of the organization. For there to be change, the engineers had to understand the desired end goal of the organization – highly satisfied customers. Their love of problem solving had to take a back seat to their commitment to the organization's goals, and so learning had to become collective.

This still did not make this company a learning organization, in that learning was still not self-generated and was organized by managers senior to the engineers. Their orientation was problem based, and learning was limited to problem solving. As a true learning organization, the engineers would become self-generating learners, and then they would be in a perfect position to discover what the designers needed to know for the next generation of products. In a true learning organization the learning can migrate in this fashion to those who can apply it best.

Learning in order to gain competitive advantage

One reason that many organizations are interested in learning is because the learning organization has a distinct competitive advantage over other types of organizations. But are the companies that are true learning organizations motivated by a thirst for competitive advantage, or is that simply part of the strategic mix? This is an important question.

Competitive advantages come and go. You may have the competitive advantage in your industry for a few years only to find that your edge disappears with the appearance of another company's product line or marketing campaign. There is a limitation to the type of learning possible when learning is motivated by the narrow goal of competitive advantages.

As we explore the make-up of true learning organizations, one thing that will become clear is the ability of these companies to take a very long look at their businesses. Several perspectives are considered simultaneously. Having an advanced, superior product may seem like a competitive advantage itself, but consider the various companies that lost out to companies with inferior products that were not as good but had better organizations that were able to make those products attractive to more people over a longer period of time.

Learning in order to gain a competitive advantage is a good idea as part of a more general learning mode. But it alone cannot be the basis for a learning organization.

Learning to ensure your own survival

Some people are of the opinion that if they do not grow, they will not survive. Learning connected with this notion results in a defensive position. Of course, when threatened by a strong competitor or by our own incompetence, the survival of the organization may, indeed, come into question. But the learning that results from this motivation will be short-lived, and once the crisis is over, the reason to learn is less immediate. As Robert Frost so aptly put it, 'I never tried to worry anyone into intelligence'. Concern about one's own survival forms a problem-driven structure. The behaviour that results tends to oscillate over time. This could hardly be the basis of a learning organization.

Learning in order to expand capacity

One of the best reasons that people join together in organizations is that the collective energies of the group can go far beyond that of any individual. Together, we can do more than we can do alone. But many people feel that their participation in an organization actually limits the expression of their talents and abilities. Some organizations bring out the best in people while others seem to bring out the worst. When people do not know how to work well together they tend to step on each other's toes. They develop strategies to compensate for the day-to-day conflicts that arise. They may withhold information, involvement, and compliance. They even may actively work against the goals of their co-workers. Within such an organization, capacity seems anything but expandable for when new people are added, the problems themselves seem to expand. The general capacity of the organization seems to reach a level of diminishing return or the overall capacity of the organization seems fixed. This is an important sign that the organization is not learning. Learning provides a chance to reorder the organization and expand its capacity.

Questions of capacity are not the same as those about specific goals. To use a simple analogy: we may want to drive at 70 miles per hour, that is our goal for speed, but this does not reflect the capacity of our engine. If our car is parked by the side of the road it continues to have the same capacity as it does when in motion. Many organizations think about capacity only when they have a problem with it. But, as in cars, as well as hi-fi speakers, amplifiers, vacuum cleaners, satellite dishes, *and organizations*, capacity affects performance.

It is wise to consider capacity issues long before complications loom on the horizon. When is it a good time to increase capacity? *When you don't need to.* Capacity can be expanded satisfactorily by anticipating the future workload. This can be done once we clearly know where we are going, where we are, and how we can move from here to there.

Expanding capacity is not limited to adding more staff or facilities to the organization. It also may and should come from streamlining. It is usually more practical to redesign systems to achieve increases in capacity than to add more resources to the same design, unless the design is at the peak of optimal performance.

Some companies do have designs that are optimal, and many can expand capacity by a system of cellular growth. McDonald's for example, expands its overall capacity by a cookie-cutter approach. Each restaurant is almost identical to the others. All the systems are standardized from location to location. Simple units, well designed for efficiency, can grow into a complex network of activity. A well-balanced system of inventory controls and distribution smoothly supports the growth of the business.

Design is essential. Part of McDonald's design contains a factor devised to anticipate what will be needed in the future. Capacity increases before business is added. McDonald's stays ahead and in touch with its future by, for example, adding low-fat items to its menu. But it also recognizes a good thing and continues to offer its very popular Big Mac.

If we are to use this principle we are required to learn by studying our businesses. We would also need the type of learning that would enable us to invent new systems and streamline procedures.

Two designs

Since organizational learning and organizational capacity are linked, and since both are affected by the business design of the company, let's take a moment to consider the issue of design. There are two basic types of business designs: *cellular* and *developmental*.

Two types of business designs

- Cellular design – franchise; cookie cutter

- Developmental design – integrated, cross-functional, systemically related: chain links

---

As we observed with McDonald's, cellular growth is generated by adding more and more independent units to the network. The success of the entire entity does not depend on the success of any individual cell, and in fact some units may fail. Yet these failures do not harm the health and well-being of the enterprise as a whole. While McDonald's distribution system is cellular, its corporate structure is developmental, in the sense that policies are created centrally for the entire organization.

Organizations which base their growth on a developmental form of business have a different relationship between the various parts of the enterprise to the whole. Each part is inextricably connected to other parts, and the organization is as strong as its weakest link. In pharmaceutical companies, for example, research and development is tied to product development, which is tied to federal regulations, which is tied to rigorous testing and documentation, which is tied to legal considerations, which is tied to marketing, which is tied to cost of development, which is tied to time to the market, which is tied to how long a patent can be owned before other companies can copy it, which is tied to finance, and so on. At any point along the chain an inadequate link can harm the business.

The learning that is required in a cellular growth business is different from that of a development growth business. In the former one can perfect small units and then multiply them. The learning may be focused on small blocks of understanding which then connect. While systems must be considered and understood, the import of this learning is less immediate. The developmental form of business requires a more rigorous understanding of systems thinking, and designs must include insight about how changes within any of the elements affect the system as a whole.

Many large organizations are attempting to change their business design from developmental to cellular by dividing each department or division into autonomous businesses. Each department competes for customers, often within the same organization. The thinking behind this type of system is that the demands of marketplace competition will drive each division to consider the internal customer, and even compete with external vendors, therefore creating a more accurate sense of reality.

For example, the type of change that is being developed at one utility company is flattening the organization into fewer levels of management (no more than six from president to lowest position), dividing each division into independent 'businesses' run with a large

---

The difference between cellular and developmental

Cellular

Developmental

- Independent units are added together

- Each unit is fundamentally related to the others

- Expansion is based on adding more and more units

- Expansion is based on a generative process and increased systemic capacity

- Success or failure of one system does not impact the total system

- It is composed of a highly integrated system in which the success of the whole is dependent on the success of each individual unit

- This design can accommodate higher levels of failure and therefore minimizes risk

- The system is organized around a targeted business strategy and maximizes workload and resource capacity ratios

- Implementation of change is difficult and the system can become inflexible

- System-wide change efforts are organized more easily

- Conflicts of interests between local success and organizational success can lead to chronic indecisiveness and business opportunities can be squandered

- Highly complex product development, business expansion, and financial management approaches can be implemented

---

degree of autonomy, but adding a newly adopted challenge of competing with outside vendors for internal customers.

This type of change can be very productive if handled well and very disruptive if not. The game has been changed radically. Many people will resist and resent the change because they are more directly responsible for producing results which make them more accountable. Their sense of risk increases. If the change is handled well a new type of organization will result that is aggressive and competitive with any outside vendor. The advantages of the type of change can be that the destiny of the organization comes into the members' hands, and marketplace reality provides accurate feedback that can help to form useful standards of measurement.

The focus on the customer, be it internal or external, can help the organization to direct its efforts to an outside frame of reference that drives the action more effectively than self-referential standards. Capacity can increase as an economy of means develops. This change of organizational design can succeed or fail. One major factor that must be adopted if it is to succeed is the learning factor. If it is motivated by a survival, then the chances of success are limited. If it is motivated by a desire to aspire to new heights of accomplishment, then success has a much greater chance. Often this type of change is driven by the wrong reasons from the start – conflict, problems, and frustration. Again, we see the impact that motivation can have on structure, and structure on learning. Motivated by conflict, the learning will stop any time the conflict is reduced. If the motivation was driven by desired end results, and formed into the context of structural tension, the learning will become an organizational habit – one that can build on itself.

When AT&T was divested many in that organization feared that they would not be able to be competitive with other long-distance phone companies. But they went to work on themselves, and changed their organization from a stodgy public monopoly to a competitive high-tech marketing organization. While the change was disruptive, perhaps it was the best change that could ever have happened to them, because they expanded their capacity through organizational learning and restructuring.

Learning in order to expand capacity is useful, and while that factor alone will not motivate a learning organization, it is an essential ingredient. As organizations begin to explore the terrain of the learning organization, new systems may be adopted that lead to change, and a good test of the efficacy of any of these new systems is their effect on capacity.

Learning so as to create desired results

Probably the best reason to learn is because we are interested in producing the results we want. The best reason for an organization to become a learning one is because of its desire for tangible goals. The goals may be specific business ones such as bringing a product to market, or they may be more general, giving customers access to a new product line or service.

More than any single motivation, the desire to create something that matters to us encourages learning at its best. The learning that takes place is highly functional and fashioned to our aspirations. It includes consistent standards of measurement established around our position in regard to a particular consequence or our skill level to produce results in the realm of our interests. It will help us to learn material, even when it is inconvenient, difficult, and complicated. It helps us to face the reality of our current abilities or conditions (which may be less desirable than we would like to admit), and from the true starting point of our competence, enables us to grow, mature, and develop.

Creating gives learning a true purpose. Organizing a company around results that matter most to the people involved can lead to an organization that has the capacity and inclination to learn. The learning is self-generating because people want to master the skills, principles, and proficiencies that will help them to accomplish their aims. They also want to learn about the current circumstances in ways that they may have avoided in the past. Habits that are a detriment are changed or overcome. People consistently rise to the occasion, and begin to learn from experience that they can count on each other.

Is this type of organization a by-product or can we attempt to create it directly? With all the excitement about learning organizations today we might get the impression that from adopting precise methods and behaviour. But that is not the case.

We can describe the characteristics of a learning organization *once* it exists, but we cannot produce a learning organization by taking on those characteristics, any more than if we looked wistfully into someone's eyes and sighed repeatedly, we could fall in love.

During Innovation Associates' (IA) Brenton Woods Conference on the learning organization, Charlie Kiefer, the founder of IA, and I did a workshop called 'The Essence Behind Learning'. At one point, we asked people to form into groups of five. We then gave them seven minutes to become 'a learning organization'. That was their only direction. They were on their own as to how they would do it. After the seven minutes were up, we asked the groups to report on what had happened. Most groups reported similar experiences: that the individuals had got to know each other and had formed a strong sense of personal relationships but that seven minutes was too short a time to create a learning organization. At first, many people did report that they had learned something, but when they were asked 'What did you learn that you didn't know before?' it turned out that they had only confirmed impressions that they already held.

Later in the workshop we gave the same-size groups an exercise that required them to create together. One member of the group was designated as the 'sculptor', the other members were 'performers', the raw materials for the piece the sculptor would create. Their job was to help the sculptor to get the result that he or she wanted.

Before the sculptors went to work we asked them to close their eyes and visualize the piece they were about to create. We asked them to form a general picture of it. 'Will it tell a story? Will it be abstract? Where are the contrasts? Where is it more active and where is it less active?' For about a minute, the sculptors formed a concept of their pieces. Once that was accomplished, we gave them two minutes to put the piece together.

After two minutes time was called and the performers held their positions. The sculptors moved away from their pieces, visited the other pieces, and then came back to their own. Then the group broke position, and another member became the sculptor. Eventually, each person had a chance to be the sculptor. The pieces were magnificent, everyone was amazed that they were able to create what they did.

During the discussion that followed this exercise people reported that, indeed, they had a tangible experience of being a learning organization or a learning group. The learning was self-generated and collective as well as individual. The learning increased over each of the two-minute projects and over the entire course of the exercise.

The contrast between the 'create a learning organization' exercise and the 'create a sculptor' exercise was dramatic. One produced a lot of talk about the learning organization, but did not create one. The other produced a learning organization, but, in this case, did so without any talk about learning.

During the 'create a sculpture' exercise the sculptors took all the steps of a creative process most commonly used by professional creators – film makers, composers, painters, novelists, and so on – in other words, *structural tension*. They began with a *general concept* of a desired end result. As they added more detail to their initial concept it evolved into a more tangible *vision*. Then they went back to their groups and observed the *current reality*: people standing around. The discrepancy between the desired state (their vision) and the actual state (the current reality) then formed a *tension*. They then took *action* as they positioned the performers as needed. How did they make decisions during this process? The actions produced chance, which they *evaluated*, using the discrepancy between the vision and reality as the standard of measurement. They then made *adjustments* as needed. This was a continual learning process – learning what worked and what didn't. They brought the piece to *completion* by adding finishing touches and asking the performers to hold their positions. This *resolved* the tension they had formed at the beginning of the process because the discrepancy between the desired state and the actual state no longer existed. They then became the *audience* for their own piece. This process, used almost universally in the arts, is also supremely well suited to organizations. To many, words like *creative process*, *creativity*, and *creating* produce images of artists starving in lofts. The reality about the creative process is that *it is the most effective process ever devised for purposes of accomplishment.* Therefore it must be practical, effective, useful, and expansive. Organizations that understand they are in the business of creating, and that therefore the creative process is their major means to accomplish their aims, are well positioned to succeed.

Overview of the creative process

The following is a review of the steps that the sculptors took in creating their pieces. The steps are a thumb-nail sketch of the process.

- *Concept* – form a general notion of the end result.
- *Vision* – frame a more specific picture of the end result.
- *Current reality* – observe the current state relevant to the desired state.
- *Action* – take strategic action designed to produce the desired outcome.
- *Evaluation* – appraise the effectiveness of the action steps that were taken.
- *Adjustment* – modify the strategy from what is learned.
- *Further action* – put the new strategy into effect, and then repeat the *evaluation–adjustment–further action* process until the project is done.

• *Completion* – add the final touches.
• *Audience* – change role from creator to end user.

Another component of the process was that the sculptors organized their actions around a time-frame and paced themselves accordingly. Most people were finished before the two minutes were even up. Their focus was on the sculpture they were creating and not on their moods, their identities, their emotions, their relationships with people, or even on how well they might do. As they worked on the sculpture they experienced a growing momentum, so that learning accelerated and actions became more effective and easier. They were fully involved. They reported two experiences of time during the exercise. One was an atmosphere of timelessness, the other was an incredible, laser-like focus on each present moment. They experienced great affinity with the other members of the group and felt that they could be counted on.

The performers also experienced a high level of involvement, growing momentum, accelerated learning, and heightened focus. During our discussion afterwards people reported that it didn't matter to them whether they were the sculptor or the performer because they were all working towards the same result. They all wanted the project to be a success. The person who originated the vision was incidental to that goal. They also experienced a sense of community with the other members of the group.

These are not sentiments commonly found among members of a corporation. Why was this short exercise able to create this type of alignment so quickly and instinctively? Because of the nature of the creative process itself. The creative process is the most successful process for accomplishing anything in the history of civilization, but, ironically, we do not get much exposure to it in either our educational systems or corporate training. Yet it would be impossible to build a learning organization without also building a creating one.

An orientation

Learning and creating are not simply activities that one does now and then. They are a way of life – an *orientation*. One reason that many organizations find it hard to embrace with any depth the prerequisite principles for becoming a learning organization is that the organization has not made a commitment to changing its fundamental way of life.

In my book, *Creating*, I make a distinction between a 'learning orientation' and a 'performing orientation'. Most of us – to the detriment of our learning process – have been educated to be *performers*. Our schools reinforce the performing orientation by rewarding us for performance *over* learning. If you do well on a test but have learned nothing, you get an 'A'. If you do not do well on a test but learn a great deal, you may get a 'C', 'D', or even an 'F'. Tradition education compensates us for high performance, not high learning.

A change of orientation is not a simple choice. It is a profound one that defines our deepest motives, values, hierarchies, as well as our truest desires. More than empty ideals, these deeper longings translate into tens of thousands of choices and actions which, taken together, define the reality of our intentions. For us to create learning organizations we may have to delve deeply into questions that we have never previously considered. This is a tall order, and yet one well worth the exploration.

Forms of learning

Learning comes in many forms. We learn from our own experiences. We also can learn vicariously from the experiences of others. We can learn intellectually, culturally, subconsciously, and intuitively. Our learning may be objective or subjective. We learn through the process of discovery and observation. We learn by experimentation, invention, and innovation. Learning can be skill based or conceptual. With so many ways to learn, it is surprising that our educational systems tend to emphasize only one – informational learning.

Many people have the idea that learning means acquiring more and more information. When they consider the concept of a 'learning' organization they envision an institution in which people are busily amassing more facts, theories, models, systems, and knowledge. It can seem overwhelming. 'It's all we can do to just do our jobs,' people who think that learning is accumulating more and more information may object. 'Who's got time to learn? And if someone does have time, how come? Perhaps they're being negligent.'

Do organizations learn in the same way individuals learn? Yes, and no. The collective learning process begins with individuals, but then it becomes more vicarious and less directly experiential. In fact, this is one of the strengths of the learning organization: That the individual learning experiences of a few people are multiplied into a more general, collective learning.

Learning myths

There are many myths about learning, and some of them restrict the dimensions of our inquiry and retard our growth.

Our brain slows down with age

The anatomy of the brain is set at gestation. As we grow older, we lose more and more of our brain cells (neurons). None are added. We have more brain cells when we are ten than when we are twenty.

During the nineteenth century many scientists believed that the size of the brain had to do with intelligence. The larger the brain, the more neurons, the more intellectual prowess we were thought to have. It became fashionable in many intellectual circles to leave one's brain to science. The brains were weighed but no consistent pattern of a size-to-intelligence ratio was found. In one report a number of professors from a great European university donated their brains to researchers. But it turned out that many of the brains actually weighed less than the norm. With a bit of reverse logic, the researchers concluded that it didn't take much intelligence to be a university professor.

A new theory was then proposed. What mattered was not the actual weight of the brain but the brain-to-body ratio. Women, the reasoning went, can be just as smart as men. They may have smaller brains but their bodies are also smaller. More brains were donated, more research was conducted, but the results were disappointing to those who held such theories. The relationship of the brain to body size did not result in any reliable predictors of intelligence.

Finally in the 1960s scientists used new high-tech microscopes to probe the brain. They discovered that while nerve cells do decrease with age, we are actually able to create more connections or paths between the remaining cells as we grow older. The networking units are called the synapses – the point where two neurons communicate. The number of synapses actually increases over time. This is why we experience being smarter at thirty than at fifteen.

Our brain not only fails to slow down with age, it can actually improve its functioning as more and more connections are made. This is why we can evolve from merely learning about specific conditions to generalizing principles of cause and effect. Our learning–information-processing abilities improve with use. As we mature, we create new sets of *self-correcting* learning strategies which enable us to expand our facilities of critical judgement.

You can learn only from experience

Many people think that they can learn only from personal experience. Certainly personal experience is a good way to learn, but it is extremely limited. As we noted earlier, one of the best ways for organizations to learn is *vicariously*. Because we are able to learn vicariously we can learn from other people's experiences as well as from our own. Technological evolution, for example, is dependent on vicarious learning. If it wasn't, every scientist, inventor, and engineer would have to personally conduct tens of thousands of experiments before they could proceed with innovative work. As it is, they can learn about these experiments in books, journals, or classes.

When the conversation turns to the learning organization vicarious learning is often left out of the discourse. But it is one of the most important factors in collective as well as personal learning. If vicarious learning is underutilized, the personal experiences of those in an organization are greatly diminished in their application, and the organization cannot increase its general knowledge base.

Learning is connected with self-concept

This myth makes learning a matter of identity. How we think of ourselves is presumed to influence our ability and interest in learning. If this myth were true how would we explain the fact that some of the most accomplished people in history had grave doubts about themselves? When we burden learning with concerns about self-esteem we confuse *who we are* with *what we want to do*. This makes learning more difficult because part of the process of learning includes making mistakes and experiencing times of incompetence and confusion. The 'feel good about yourself' movement in education and elsewhere inadvertently devalues the desire to learn by assuming that the reason people do what they do is to enhance self-esteem.

If that were the case, then learning would only be a ploy designed to bolster one's ego, and its intrinsic value would be incidental.

Learning is hard enough. But when issues of identity are added, people become overly sensitive to how they deal with mistakes, personal inadequacies, and temporary gaps in their understanding or abilities. We are in a better position to learn when we perceive the learning situation for what it actually is: a situation in which we are improving, exploring, grappling with new understanding, and adding to our level of competence. We are imperfect beings with a lot to learn. Our imperfections will not be taken personally during the learning process when we keep our identities out of it.

Learning is more of the same

When we think about learning we often assume that future learning will be the same as the learning that we have done in the past. In doing this we often miss out on types of learning that are new or atypical. Many people approach new learning situations with outdated habits, thereby limiting the possibility of opening new vistas. Can we be taught 'new tricks' or are we like 'old dogs'? With the advent of computers, many people became learners anew; the type of learning that was required of them was different from that they had previously experienced.

It is hard to introduce a new approach to learning into organizations because so many companies attempt to force new concepts, abilities, and methods into outmoded learning patterns. For many innovations, part of the essential learning is not the content of what is being learned but *how* to learn this new content.

Learning is permanent

One myth that many of us subscribe to is that once we learn something, we know it for good. This is not always true. Many skills must be updated in order for us to stay current within our fields. Some basic 'truths' may be proved incorrect or become obsolete. Part of the instinct or habit of the learning organization is to stay current with those understandings that constitute the governing ideas of a company. This may be technical information, management styles, thinking skills, business strategies, and marketing approaches. It may also be the fundamental purpose of the organization, the values it holds, the vision to which it aspires, and its reasons to exist. All of these may need to be reconceived as a company evolves.

We are better positioned to learn if we make the assumption that what we know is subject to continual questioning. Then we are less likely to build in assumptions that may prove to be limiting. The same principle is true for organizations.

Learning guidelines

The following are a list of guidelines that can make learning, especially learning in an organizational setting, easier to accomplish.

Keep the desired goal of the learning in mind

What motivates us to learn? The answer may vary from person to person, from organization to organization, and from situation to situation. But whatever the motivation, it is best to always keep it in mind so that we can focus our efforts and tailor our means. Furthermore, it is effective to know not only the purpose of the learning but also the more general ends the learning serves. Is it to encourage product development or managerial design? Is it to increase profitability or market position? Is it to improve quality or the speed of delivery? When we keep the learning goal in mind we are more able to approach learning with an economy of means, emphasizing what we need and de-emphasizing what we don't.

Communicate the desired end result to others

Once we are clear about our purpose in learning, let others know. The major group of people to communicate with is, of course, the people directly involved with the learning goal. But it is useful to let other people in the organization know as well. It may result in important discussions that may not have otherwise occurred. Out of this communication we can involve others in our thought processes and join together in collective learning. This adds insight, clarity, and perspective to our cause. These types of interactions are an important part of organizational learning, our co-exploration of fundamental issues increases our understanding, both individually and collectively. It also increases our capacity and habit to learn from each other.

When we are clear about our learning goals and communicate those goals to others, we benefit in at least four major ways:

1 We elicit help in the form of conversation and/or support.
2 We become clearer ourselves.
3 We are able to create clear standards of measurement we can use in evaluating our progress.
4 We gain the perspective of other people's viewpoints.

Explore reality rather than advocate positions

With the advent of the learning organization many people have seized the opportunity to promote their particular methodology or philosophy of life. Learning, to them, means 'learning what I have to teach you'. A learning organization, to them, would be an organization that holds *their* beliefs and adopts their processes. The tendency to use learning as a chance to proselytize can confuse a rather complicated subject.

Learning is best accomplished by a process of true inquiry rather than by advocating one's own beliefs. In inquiry, *everything is up for grabs*. Every assumption and 'truth' can be rethought and scrutinized. In inquiry, we start with nothing, that is, we begin our exploration independent of our preconceptions. Questions are more than rhetorical arguments.

The term *dialogue* as used by David Bohem and Peter Senge means co-exploring and co-discovering. Some people use *dialogue* to mean that we should listen to their assertions without critical judgement. True inquiry, however, is different from considering everything indiscriminately. With true inquiry, we are able to penetrate the subject matter with enhanced critical judgement. That is a skill that the learning organization depends on and which will be developed in the next chapter.

7   Thinking

All of us have been taught to think *comparatively*. We acquire facts, theories, experiences, speculations, and information. When we regard reality, we *compare* what we see with our pre-existing database. We are able to identify specific objects, experiences, or situations by comparing their similarities and differences with general categories of corresponding objects, experiences, or situations.

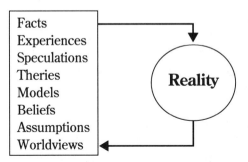

Facts
Experiences
Speculations
Theries
Models
Beliefs
Assumptions
Worldviews

Reality

This process is useful in helping us to negotiate the world. If we see a cat we do not need to rediscover what it is. We can classify the animal based on our experience and knowledge of cats in general. We assume that the characteristics that are true of the general group are also true of this cat in particular. Because we know something about cats we can position ourselves in a relationship to a cat we have never seen before. If we have had favourable experiences with cats we might welcome the encounter. If we have had disagreeable experiences we might avoid it. Our reactions, attitudes, and responses are determined largely by what we already know.

Through comparative thinking, we observe qualities that are *common* to the group but *different* for a specific individual. While we recognize that a particular cat is *similar* to all other cats, we also identify the *unique* aspects of that particular cat.

We can also put *similar* attributes into *different categories* when necessary. A very large cat may be a mountain lion. The mountain lion shares many characteristics with the house cat, but the differences tell us that this is not Tabby, and that it may not treat us with the same degree of affection.

Since comparative thinking is the most common thought process, many of our learning systems are built upon the assumption that we need to accumulate or access knowledge. Learned people know a great deal. Are they learned because they can *think* or because they can *associate* what they know already to what they see? Too often the emphasis is on the latter.

Many people, in and out of organizations, use comparative thinking *exclusively*. They categorize reality. When it is said that one is 'thinking differently', all that is meant is that a new basis for comparison has been adopted and a previous one abandoned. The process is still the same; the only change is that new categories are now thought to be true.

Encountering unfamiliar conditions

Comparative thinking is convenient but limited, particularly when we encounter *new* situations. We tend to assume that the new situation is similar to others we have already experienced or know about. Once we identify a new situation as similar to another, we bring in an entire set of assumptions into play. We import our convictions, preconceptions, biases, propensities, persuasions, and theories, *and impose them on the new condition*. They may not hold true, however. We may conclude that we know much more than we do. And how can we explore and learn when we are busy making the assumption that we already know?

Thinking

Thinking is more than simply perceiving reality and then comparing our observations with our database. It is more than merely categorizing. To think is to *observe, separate, fuse,* and *assemble.* It's also to:

- *Generalize* – to form generic shapes from singular events or patterns
- *Individualize* – to establish a distinct classification for each new phenomenon
- *Systematize* – to create a sequence of levels, degrees, or steps
- *Conceive* – to imagine, suppose, visualize
- *Extrapolate* – to extend the direction of tendencies, so we can envision various outcomes based on past sequences or patterns
- *Contrast* – to form differences

Relationships

Most importantly, thinking is the ability to *construct relationships among the various elements that are being considered* and then to *generate new sets of relationships.* Perhaps the greatest faculty of thought is that of organizing information into sets of relationships. These relationships give us an impression of understanding and a sense of orientation. We are able to know what the elements of a situation are, how they function, and how they impact each other.

Relational sets

One level of explanation about the world is that individual events are caused by other individual events.

$$\text{Event} \longrightarrow \text{Event} \longrightarrow \text{Event}$$

We often link a current event to other events in a chain. Why did the market share go down (event)? Because the price of the product went up (previous event). Why did the price go up (event)? Because the price of oil rose (another previous event). Why? Because of a world shortage of oil (another previous event).

While events do, in fact, *seem* to cause other events the type of thinking that is produced by this explanation limits us to reacting against or responding to each individual event. Do we truly understand what causes the *series* of events from this explanation? No. We only know that each is connected to another. Consequently, we are unable to alter the course of the sequence as it plays itself out.

Another set of relationships that describes the series of events is the pattern. Patterns are repeated sequences. The nature of patterns is that we can recognize the entire series of events as they follow in sequence.

When we are able to recognize patterns, we can predict future events in a sequence before they have occurred, and in so doing, we can anticipate our response. This gives us a sense of more understanding from which we can organize our actions. Unfortunately, it does not give us the ability to *change* the patterns, because still we do not understand what *causes* the pattern.

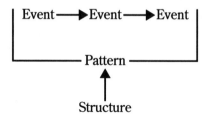

Events and patterns are formed by underlying structures – *relationships that create tendencies for movement and change*. When we think structurally, not only are we observing individual elements, events, and patterns but we are also exploring sets of relationships that give rise to tendencies for behaviour that are inherent in those relationships. Not only can we understand that a predictable pattern of oscillation is taking place, we can also understand the structural conflicts that cause it to happen. Furthermore, we can restructure the forces in play so that we are better able to produce the behaviour we desire, as we do when we restructure a structural conflict to structural tension.

We have not been taught to think in terms of causal structures. Yes, we form relationships in our mental processes, but we usually form these connections inadvertently and haphazardly – typically based on previous associations compared with current situations – a 'this reminds me of that' type of reaction. We then trigger relational sets that appear to connect. This triggering gives an illusory sense of understanding and orientation. We have an explanation, and that makes us feel better, even though we still do not know what is causing the current conditions.

Without understanding of how to think structurally we are unlikely to effect real and lasting change in our organizations and in our lives. All we can do is react or respond to circumstances, or anticipate future ones. *We will be unable to generate what we want, independent of the circumstances.*

Our organizations and lives are products of countless structural interactions that are often invisible until we search them out. But we are unable to find them when we do not know how to look.

Thinking in structures

Structural thinking does not use models of reality, theories of human behaviour, intuition, free association, *or any other previously learned notions.* Instead, we begin without preconception. We begin with *nothing.* We then make observations about reality, and from those observations, understand the internal relationships that create cause and effect. Even the models of structural tension and structural conflict are better *discovered* by observing reality, rather than imposing them on reality. If these relationships actually exist, they will become obvious. If they do not, there is no need to pretend they do.

In the early 1980s I developed and began teaching a particular method for structural thinking that consultants could use in their work. Soon, many managers began to attend our training sessions as well, because the skills the consultants were learning were directly applicable to management utilization. The new approach was unique and in some way the antithesis of the model-based approaches most of these people had been using. I called this approach *Structural Consulting.*

Structural consulting

Most consulting methods begin with a model, theory, or set of past experiences that is used to diagnose conditions. Once the client's conditions are categorized, prescriptions for changes are proposed. Although the nature of theories or experiences may vary widely from consultant to consultant, and from method to method, the *form* of thinking is identical – *comparative.*

Structural Consulting is a method that enables clients to deeply understand the forces in play in any situation, and take effective strategic action designed to create desired outcomes. Often reality is obscured by faulty information, inaccurate assumptions, and a misunderstanding of the structures in play. Through Structural Consulting the consultant and client *authentically co-explore reality objectively* amid the spirit of true inquiry.

The method begins with a 'blank sheet of paper', so to speak. Rather than beginning with a theory or set of previous experiences, the consultant begins *without* preconceptions.

Through a series of questions that are natural outcomes of the information that the client presents, the situation becomes clear. As the picture fills in, the client is able to gain new perspectives about reality.

The consulting process produces an essential understanding of the cause-and-effect relationships that are occurring, and the client is positioned to make strategic choices, take effective action, or develop needed adjustments.

Because Structural Consulting examines reality outside the frame of preconceived notions, both consultant and client are able to look at the situation *freshly* and *originally*. The results of this perspective naturally lead us to consider a broader structural and systemic perception.

Additive picturing

In order to help people to learn this new thinking process I developed a technique I call *additive picturing*. Through it, we are *translating information we are receiving into a visual language*, and then *adding each additional picture to previous pictures we form*. At first the pictures might seem like a montage of loosely related or even unrelated images. Soon, however, *internal* commonalties and differences begin to appear. When we perceive information visually, relationships between elements often become obvious to us. Structures begin to appear, and causal relationships often become apparent.

Steps in additive picturing

1 *Start with nothing.* This is probably the most difficult step for most people first learning this skill. Is it possible to view reality without a past frame of reference? Yes. If we were accountants we would not tackle a new tax form by saying 'You know, this tax form reminds of one I did a few days ago. Why don't I just move right to the bottom line and fill in the numbers that I used the other day!' No amount of previous experience would permit the accountant to bypass observing the actual numbers.

The skill of starting a thought process without preconceptions or biases can be developed with practice. We can avoid our tendency to jump to association when we limit our frame of reference to our observations and only our observations. Part of the discipline of this approach is that the consultant never presumes information that has not been observed.

2 *Listen to what is being said.* The client describes the current situation.

3 *Form pictures of the information.* Perhaps the client says 'I climbed a tree Saturday morning at nine-thirty'. We form a picture of that person climbing a tree. Information that is not translatable to a pictorial form needs better definition, so we ask questions until we can form a picture of it.

4 *Add each new picture to the other pictures.* At first, the pictures may seem simply to be information that is unrelated. As we get more information, the pictures begin to form groupings. Clusters of relationships may then appear, and eventually deeper structural relationships emerge.

5 *Identify discrepancies.* As we listen, form and add pictures, we will begin to observe discrepancies between two or more pictures.

6 *Ask questions to explain discrepancies.* There are only two possibilities when sorting out discrepancies: either one or both of the points of information is inaccurate, or there is some additional information you do not have that explains the apparent discrepancy. For example, perhaps our client tells us 'I climbed a tree Saturday morning at nine-thirty', but later tells us 'I went home Saturday morning at nine-thirty'. We have a picture of the client climbing a tree and going home during the same time period. This forms an apparent discrepancy. How are we to explain the apparent discrepancy? Too often, when we are faced with this type of

discrepancy our tendency is to invent an explanation because we do not feel comfortable with dissonance. Also the habit of jumping to associations may be so ingrained in us that we may not know that we have added an explanation of our own. We may presume that we know what we don't actually know by filling in our concept of what *might* have happened. The discrepancy will then become more obscure, and we will have the impression that we understand more than we do. Did the person go to climb the tree or go home? There is a limited number of possibilities.

One statement is true, the other isn't

The statement 'I climbed a tree Saturday morning at nine-thirty' may be true, and the other statement 'I went home on Saturday morning at nine-thirty' untrue, or vice versa. Or both may be inaccurate. We can ask questions that are focused on explaining the discrepancy. The answers can point to which statement is accurate and which is not. Rather than an adversarial police type of investigation, the consultant and client work together. 'How are we to explain this discrepancy?'

In a long conversation about complicated organizational issues many discrepancies will emerge. Often they are lost by a 'short hand' comparative thought process, and much information that is valuable to have on the table is taken off the table by conjecture. This practice dulls our awareness of the discrepancy. Yet we want to know of the existence of prevailing discrepancies so that we can understand the forces that are really in play by asking relevant questions.

The following is the only other possibility that explains the discrepancy.

There is information that we do not have that explains the discrepancy

The other possibility is that both statements are true, but there is information that we need to explain the apparent discrepancy. 'I climbed a tree and went home on Saturday morning at nine-thirty because I live in a tree-house.' The new information (home is in a tree) explains the situation, which no longer contains a discrepancy.

The technique of additive picturing helps us to keep our own biases out of the exploration, because it limits the information to pictures based on what the client has said. There is no room to import our own preconceptions. The visual translation forces us to make the information we are receiving tangible rather than abstract.

Many people mix elements such as fact, theories about what caused the situation, how to solve it, who to blame, and why it shouldn't have happened with their description of reality. Sorting out fact from the other elements can help to make objective reality distinct from subjective reality. During the consultation both client and consultant experience a cooperative learning spirit as objective reality becomes clearer. The greater perspective enables the client to better understand underlying structures, and what approach might be adopted.

Many managers have used this approach with the people they manage, and it has enabled the group to rethink many of the assumptions that were built into their companies, divisions, departments, and teams, and adjust or redesign as needed.

We can use this thought process ourselves by playing both client and consultant roles. For people just learning this skill this can be a bit difficult, but after some experience, new perceptions can be reached. Greater insight helps in our decision-making process because we can move from the event level of concern to a structural level of understanding.

In the consulting I have done within organizations most people begin with event-level perceptions but later reach valuable structural insights that change their abilities to deal with complicated issues.

Thinking in groups

One of the great benefits of Structural Consulting and the thinking that it produces is that a group of people can co-explore reality as easily as an individual. In fact, it is often easier to work with a group because there are more sources of information available, particularly when the exploration is conducted by an experienced structural consultant.

Of course, at the beginning of the exploration everyone has his or her own opinion about reality, usually expressed in an event-level explanation. By starting without preconception, and then translating information into visual forms, adding the pictures together, sorting out discrepancies, and testing our assumptions, fantastic insights become clear to everyone.

We learn many lessons about the authentic structure that is giving rise to the events we are witnessing, how our actions may or may not contribute to our desired end results, what those desired outcomes are, how to support what matters to us, what our collective values are, how to work together rather than against each other, and so on. We also learn general lessons about the process of learning together through exploring reality, rather than people simply insisting on their individual viewpoints. We learn that reality may not truly be what we assumed it was.

When faced with a discrepancy, human beings have an instinct to act. We want to resolve it. Unfortunately, *our tendency is to act before we understand.* Sometimes our reactions seem to work, at least temporarily. But too often our actions turn out to work against our legitimate longer-term desires.

When we act fast our feeling is one of control and power. We feel in charge of circumstances, and we rejoice in our expeditious responses. But our instincts often mislead us. We can act based on inadequate information, perceptions, or habits.

We need to study reality more astutely than we usually do. Not only that, we need to equip ourselves with better instruments for our investigation. Comparative thought processes inherently contain an element in which free association connects points of data, and gives us the illusion of deeper understanding.

Some people think that if we deliberate over a longer period of time our results will be more successful. This notion is seldom accurate. Longer deliberation, but still using inadequate methods, doesn't significantly alter the ability to penetrate the structures that are causal. There is no real difference if the only change we make is to jump to conclusions slowly rather than quickly – we would still be jumping to conclusions.

Wisdom does not often express itself through reaction or response, but through a disciplined thought process *that allows us to go beyond our previously assumed truths.* The same principle is true when we work together in teams and organizations.

When groups of people jump to various conclusions they may argue with each other about whose conclusion is correct. Little progress is made but some adversity is created. Camps of opinions form and controversies may become political in nature. No one is to blame, however, because this type of situation is the natural byprod-uct of the exclusive use of comparative thinking and the inability to think originally. Anyone faced with the same kind of stimuli and ill-equipped to go beyond old thought processes, naturally will end up in the same situation.

What makes this type of occurrence more deeply ingrained in our organizations is that often people have created their past success using these same types of thought process. It is hard to argue with success. But new situations will not yield to the outdated thought processes of the past, and time works against us as we attempt to forge a new future.

New challenges are not past challenges, and are not always addressable through past experiences. So-called 'open discussions' fail to lead to new insights because merely sharing opinions fails to provide a collective process of exploration. Well-meaning people try their best, but they are left with a tapestry of opinions that do not lend essential understanding about how these opinions came about.

Of course, people are always able to point to aspects of reality to substantiate their ideas. But often reality continues on unstudied and unexplored.

People try to change, but too often they are offered only substitutes in the basis of comparisons. We are encouraged to change our models, theories, ideals, methods, systems, and views. This type of change does not lead to a change of thought process but rather to variations on the theme of comparison. Progress seems not to last, and unhappily, people return to business as usual.

Learning is inextricably tied to thinking. To attempt to generate a learning organization from an inadequate comparative thought process fails to reach the noble aspirations that are truly desired. We must rethink our processes of thought so that we can learn what we do not currently know.

Rethinking the organization

When we attempt to think about our organizations we often fall into traps of fixed notions and ideas. Then we use comparative thinking and problem solving to find our way out of inadequate organizational conditions. This type of process only serves to entrench us more deeply in our structural designs. More of the same type of thinking that created the conditions will lead only to duplicating the conditions later. So we need to rethink our organizations, but we also need to rethink how we think about them. As we master the principles of structural thinking, new ideas become available, new concepts are advanced, and new possibilities are born.

Epilogue: Change

How can we change our organizations? By understanding that our ultimate motive to change is so that we can build, originate, form, organize, invent, produce, and create; rather than to fix problems, eradicate obstacles, and solve the dilemmas. Too often, organizational change efforts are rooted in a fear of negative consequences rather than in glorious aspirations and deeply held values. The motive will set the direction. Is it to bring into being the type of organization we want, or is it to eliminate what we don't want?

We can change our organizations by changing the way we think (how we process information, make observations, understand relationships systemically and structurally, and understand how the various elements combine to structural tendencies) – not simply *what* we think (the content, our conclusions, our concepts, and so on).

Many of today's change methods do not attempt to modify the *way* we think, but simply *what* we think. New prescriptions, new tricks, new manipulative ploys, new warm and fuzzy philosophies, new pep talks, new jargon cannot succeed for long. Each change effort is followed by another, and then another. Change becomes disruptive rather than helpful. Why is it so popular to take on these methods given their lack of eventual success? Because they don't take a lot of thought. They might take a lot of work, a lot of talk, a lot of data gathering and analysis, a lot of rearrangement of systems, strategies, and people. They may even take a lot of mental work, but not a lot of thought.

A successful change in thinking method moves from a comparative to an original process. When we think we know, we do not look as carefully at reality. We think we see what isn't there, and we miss what is.

A successful change in thinking method is preceded by a change in *why* we look at reality. The point of our usual organizational thought process is to *change* a condition rather than *understand* it. While subtle, this is a useful distinction.

If we were attempting to understand a condition only so that we could change it, we would focus our level of observation on what is wrong. We would find various symptoms. We would then define the symptoms as problems. This would lead us to construct a solution that is tailored to the problem description. If we said that the problem was that people were not making decisions or generating new systems or ideas, we would give them empowerment training. If we said that quality was inadequate, put in a total quality programme. If we said that profits were declining, beef up sales, lower costs, and raise the price. The way the problem is defined biases the action. The time-frame is short, immediate, just where we, as managers, want it so we can take decisive action. Because we want to control the outcomes, we look for those procedures we can use right away. After all, we are compensated for taking charge and acting.

Multiply this thought process throughout the organization, and suddenly the air is filled with crisis and chaos. There is no shortage of solutions. But they seem not to work. Everyone has a pet theory about what's going on as the symptoms get a lot of attention, but their causes are ignored.

The other motive is that we study the conditions so that we can better understand what causes them. While this information will prove itself to be immensely useful once we attempt to move in the direction we want to go, at the outset it is best simply to understand what is truly causing the effects we are observing. Like the scientist who studies the workings of the genetic code of a virus to understand what causes the virus to behave as it does, even though the study, if successful, will be used to create new approaches to address the virus, we must enter our study of reality first to understand, not to eliminate or change it.

The questions we use to observe reality are different. When we try to fix or solve, we ask 'How do we stop the condition?' or 'How do we get away from the condition?' When we study reality to understand what causes it, we might ask 'How are we to understand what is going on?' or 'What are the forces in play that generate this situation?' Because the questions are different, the answers will be different. The first set of questions will lead to describing symptoms and the second to observing relationships. These observations may lead to more questions that yield more observations that lead to more questions, and so on, until we understand the structural relationships that exist among the forces which give rise to the behavioural tendencies that exist.

Studying reality positions us to understand better the forces in play, which is useful when we want to accomplish an overriding purpose as we often do in organizations. Understanding causes of the current condition does not lead to generating our purpose and goals. But when combined, we are able to organize our actions through the frame of structural tension: the desired state/actual state relationship.

Multiply this thought process throughout an organization and we have people able to join together in a concerted effort rather than individuals acting as lone agents attempting to search for and destroy the problems. In such an organization the conversations people have are useful explorations that help to penetrate the true causes of conditions, as well as shared aspirations and visions for the future. This is in sharp contrast to organizations in which people advocate positions to each other, and then become upset if others remain unconvinced.

If we are motivated by aspiration, and we can think independently of our theoretical or experiential biases, we have the bases of structural tension. We can organize change functionally. What has to change so that we can better create our goals? What do we have in place currently in relationship to those goals? How are we to understand the forces in play? These questions can lead to deciding what our hierarchy is concerning our goals, strategies, values, and purpose. No matter how fragmented an organization is, there will be certain thematic unifying principles that everyone will share. The purpose is one such principle. So is a comprehensive business strategy. So is a clear and comprehensive management strategy. Another unifying principle is the ability to observe reality from both the details and the shapes and patterns the details form.

The nature of change is the same as the nature of the status quo. The underlying structure will determine the ultimate behaviour. Organizations that complain that change is hard because people have an aversion to change miss seeing why people in their organizations have such an aversion while those in other organizations do not. Do they simply hire a different sort of person or are there causal reasons for the difference? The work we have done within organizations over the past twenty or so years has demonstrated that change is an outcome of the structural design of the company. The major type of change that we consider a great success is when the organization moves from a pattern of oscillation between competing forces to one of resolving behaviours in which goals are accomplished, and these become the basis of new growth and development. The only time this type of change occurs organizationally is when the change is made on a structural level of the organization's architecture. That is why we have stressed the relationship of structure to organizational performance in this book. This is an unusual insight in an age in which people are not trained to think in structural terms. But it is an essential insight for us to fulfil our dynamic urge to build the future we want.

Bibliography

Benson, Tracey E. (1992) 'Industry's unsung heroes: Mark W. Snowberger', *Industry Week*, 7 December, pp. 34–35

Binney, George *et al.* (1992) *Making Quality Work – lessons from Europe's leading companies*, The Economist Intelligence Unit, London

Bronowski, Jacob (1973) *The Ascent of Man*, BBC Publications, London

Fritz, Robert (1994) *The Path of Least Resistance*, 2nd edition, Butterworth-Heinemann, Oxford

Fritz, Robert (1994) *Creating*, Butterworth-Heinemann, Oxford

Gabor, Andrea (1990) *The Man Who Discovered Quality*, Times Books, New York

Hamel, Gary and Prahalad, C.K. (1989) 'Strategic intent', *Harvard Business Review*, May–June, **67**(3), pp. 63–76

Kaufman, Robert S. (1992) 'Why operations improvement programs fail: for managerial contradictions', *Sloan Management Review* (Fall), **34**(1), pp. 83–93

Peters, Tom and Waterman, N.H. (1983) *In Search of Excellence*, Collins, London

Senge, Peter (1991) *The Fifth Discipline: The art and practice of the learning organisation*, Century Business, London

Training and Development (1993) January, p. 4

We hope you have enjoyed this book and have found the concepts and principles of value. If you would like more information about the **Technologies for Creating®** curriculum and the courses, programs, products and consulting services offered, you may reach us at:

UK Head Office:

Chloe Cox Consultants Ltd
2 Castle Street, Stroud
Gloucestershire GL5 2HP
England
Phone (+44) 145 376 5585
Fax (+44) 145 375 6054

UK Offices:

Lerner Baird Associates
13 Poets Road, London N5 2SL
England
Phone and fax (+44) 171 359 1495

Glyn Williams
93C Priory Road, London N8 8LY
England
Phone (+44) 181 341 3556

Frances Barnett
West Hall, Parracombe
Barnstable, Devon EX31 4PF
England
Phone and fax (+44) 1598 736 3384

Alan Mossman
19 Whitehall, Stroud
Gloucestershire GL5 1HA
England
Phone (+44) 145 376 5611
Fax (+44) 145 375 6054

International Office:

Technologies for Creating®
Box 116, Grimes Hill Road
Williamsville, Vermont, USA 05362.011
Phone 802 348 7176 or 800 848 9700
Fax 802 348 7444

Thank you for your interest.

Index